CLIFFS  W9-AKL-496

Law School Admission Test

PREPARATION GUIDE

by

Peter Z. Orton, M.Ed.

Consultants

Thomas P. Wolfe, Ph.D.
Rich Michaels, M.A.
Howard Horwitz, M.A.

Cliffs Notes

INCORPORATED

LINCOLN, NEBRASKA   68501

ACKNOWLEDGMENTS

The author would like to thank Michele Spence of Cliffs Notes for final editing and careful attention to the production process and typist Lynne Turner for exceptional work in preparing the manuscript.

The author would also like to thank his parents, William and Esta Orton, for their continued support and love through the years.

CONTENTS

iii

PART III: PRACTICE-REVIEW-ANALYZE-PRACTICE
Two Full-Length Practice Tests

PREFACE

YOUR LSAT SCORE WILL MAKE THE DIFFERENCE! And thorough preparation can help you do your best! This LSAT study guide is direct, precise, and easy to use. The comprehensive test preparation program can be carefully completed in a reasonable time and provides everything you need to do your best on the LSAT. The strategies and materials presented in this guide have been researched, tested, and evaluated in actual LSAT preparation classes.

This guide also features the PATTERNED PLAN OF ATTACK for each section while focusing on:

1. The Ability Tested
2. The Basic Skills Necessary
3. Understanding Directions
4. Analysis of Directions
5. Suggested Approach with Samples
6. Practice-Review-Analyze-Practice

This LSAT study guide includes two complete LSAT practice exams—similar to the actual LSAT in question types and time allotments—with answers and in-depth explanations.

Cliffs LSAT Preparation Guide was written to give you maximum return on your investment of study time. Follow the Study Guide Checklist and work through this book systematically. It will give you the edge to do your best!

STUDY GUIDE CHECKLIST

_____ 1. Read the LSAT Information Bulletin and Sample Test included in your Registration Packet.

_____ 2. Become familiar with the Test Format, page 3.

_____ 3. Familiarize yourself with the answers to Questions Commonly Asked about the LSAT, page 5.

_____ 4. Learn the techniques of Two Successful Overall Approaches, page 7.

_____ 5. Carefully read Part II: Analysis of Exam Areas, beginning on page 11.

_____ 6. Strictly observing time allotments, take Practice Test 1, section by section (review answers after each section), beginning on page 51.

_____ 7. Check your answers and analyze your results, beginning on page 123.

_____ 8. Fill out the Tally Sheet for Problems Missed to pinpoint your mistakes, page 126.

_____ 9. While referring to each item of Practice Test 1, study ALL the Answers and Complete Explanations, beginning on page 127.

_____ 10. Review as necessary the Analysis of Exam Areas, beginning on page 11.

_____ 11. Strictly observing time allotments, take Practice Test 2, section by section (review answers after each section), beginning on page 153.

_____ 12. Check your answers and analyze your results, beginning on page 219.

_____ 13. Fill out the Tally Sheet for Problems Missed to pinpoint your mistakes, page 222.

_____ 14. While referring to each item of Practice Test 2, study ALL the Answers and Complete Explanations, beginning on page 223.

_____ 15. Carefully reread Part II: Analysis of Exam Areas, beginning on page 11.

_____ 16. Go over Final Preparation, page 247.

Part I: Introduction

FORMAT OF THE NEW LSAT EXAM

Section	Subject Area (order will vary)	Time	Number of Questions
	Essay	30 Minutes	
I	Reading Comprehension	35 Minutes	27–29
II	Analytical Reasoning	35 Minutes	23–25
III	Dispute Characterization	35 Minutes	35–40
IV	Logical Reasoning	35 Minutes	25–27
V	Experimental	35 Minutes	varies
VI	Experimental	35 Minutes	varies

Total Time: 210 minutes = 3½ hours (plus ½ hour for writing the essay)

Approximately 170 questions (110–120 questions actually count toward your score)

IMPORTANT NOTE: The order in which the sections appear and the number of questions in each section may vary because there are several forms of the new LSAT. *The experimental sections may appear at any point in the test,* and each will probably repeat one of the common sections.

GENERAL DESCRIPTION

The LSAT lasts 4 hours: 3½ hours of multiple-choice questions plus a 30-minute unscored essay. All questions are of equal value. The test is scored from 10 to 48. The sections are:

ESSAY—You will be asked to write a clear, concise essay on a topic provided. The essay will not be graded, but a copy will be sent along with your test score to your prospective law schools.

READING COMPREHENSION—You will answer questions about reading passages from a variety of subject areas. Referring back to the passage is permitted.

ANALYTICAL REASONING—You will derive information and deduce spatial and other relationships from groups of conditions or statements.

DISPUTE CHARACTERIZATION—You will evaluate questions based on a sequence of facts, a dispute, and a pair of rules.

LOGICAL REASONING—You will derive logical conclusions and relationships from a variety of situations and passages.

These common sections and the essay question will require no specific knowledge from any specialized course or courses. No formal background in law is required or necessary.

QUESTIONS COMMONLY ASKED
ABOUT THE LSAT

Q: WHO ADMINISTERS THE LSAT?

A: The Law School Admission Test is administered by Law School Admission Services, Inc. If you wish any information not covered in this book, write to Law School Admission Services, Box 2000, Newtown, PA 18940.

Q: CAN I TAKE THE LSAT MORE THAN ONCE?

A: You may repeat the LSAT, but be advised that your prospective law school(s) will receive all your scores, along with the advice that the average score may be the most accurate indication of your achievement.

Q: WHAT MATERIALS MAY I BRING TO THE LSAT?

A: Bring your admission ticket/identification card with a 2½" × 2½" color closeup photo of yourself (the photo will not be returned), two positive identifications (with picture, descriptive information, etc.), a watch, three or four sharpened Number 2 pencils, and a good eraser. A pen for writing the essay will be provided at the exam. You may not bring scratch paper or books. You may plan your essay using the scratch paper provided and rely on the space provided in the test booklet for scratch work during the objective test.

Q: IF NECESSARY, MAY I CANCEL MY SCORE?

A: Yes. You may cancel your score by notifying the test center supervisor on the day of the test or by sending a mailgram to LSAS within five days of the test date. Your LSAT score report will note that you have canceled a score and have seen the test questions.

Q: SHOULD I GUESS ON THE LSAT?

A: Yes. There is no penalty for guessing on the LSAT. Before taking a wild guess, remember that eliminating one or more of the choices increases your chances of choosing the right answer.

Q: HOW SHOULD I PREPARE FOR THE LSAT?

A: Because knowledge of particular subject matter is not necessary for the LSAT, the mastery of test-taking strategies will contribute most successfully to a good score. Courses involving critical thinking, reading comprehension, writing, and simple logic can also be helpful.

Q: WHEN IS THE LSAT ADMINISTERED?

A: The LSAT is administered four times during the school year, in October, December, February, and June. Three of these administrations will probably occur on Saturday mornings, beginning at 8:30 A.M., and one administration may occur on a Monday afternoon (usually June administration).

Q: WHERE IS THE LSAT ADMINISTERED?

A: The LSAT is administered at a number of colleges and universities worldwide. A list of testing centers is included in the LSAT/LSDAS Registration Packet, published by LSAS.

Q: HOW AND WHEN SHOULD I REGISTER?

A: Complete registration materials are included in the LSAT/ LSDAS Registration Packet, available free at the Office of Testing or Graduate Studies at your university or from most law schools. To register, mail in the forms provided, along with the appropriate fees. You should register at least five weeks prior to the exam date.

Q: WHAT IS LSDAS?

A: The Law School Data Assembly Service collects the necessary information for your application to law school, arranges it into the standardized format preferred by many law schools, and mails it upon the applicant's request. Registration material for the LSDAS is provided in the LSAT/LSDAS Registration Packet.

Q: HOW DOES THE PRESENT LSAT DIFFER FROM PAST ADMINISTRATIONS?

A: Before June, 1982, the LSAT included math sections (Quantitative Comparison and Data Interpretation) and an objective test of "Writing Ability," as well as Practical Judgment and Cases and Principles sections. All of these sections have been removed from the test, and the variable time limits of past sections have been replaced with a uniform 35-minute limit on each section. The only section from the pre-June LSAT that still remains, in somewhat altered form, is Logical Reasoning. No math problems remain on the present test, and the objective Writing Ability sections (Error Recognition/Sentence Correction/Usage) have been replaced with a 30-minute unscored essay question.

TAKING THE LSAT: TWO SUCCESSFUL OVERALL APPROACHES

Many who take the LSAT don't get their best score because they spend too much time dwelling on hard questions, leaving insufficient time to answer the easy questions they can get right. Don't let this happen to you. Use the following system to mark your answer sheet:

I. The "Plus-Minus" Strategy

1. Answer easy questions immediately.
2. Place a "+" next to any problem that seems solvable but is too time-consuming, take a guess, and go on to the next question.
3. Place a "−" next to any problem that seems impossible. Act quickly. Don't waste time deciding whether a problem is a "+" or a "−." Then take a guess and move on.

After working all the problems you can do immediately, go back and work your "+" problems. If you finish them, try your "−" problems (sometimes when you come back to a problem that seemed impossible you will suddenly realize how to solve it).

Your answer sheet should look something like this after you finish working your easy questions:

```
 1. Ⓐ ● Ⓒ Ⓓ Ⓔ
+2. Ⓐ Ⓑ Ⓒ ● Ⓔ
 3. Ⓐ Ⓑ ● Ⓓ Ⓔ
−4. ● Ⓑ Ⓒ Ⓓ Ⓔ
+5. Ⓐ Ⓑ Ⓒ ● Ⓔ
```

Make sure to erase your "+" and "−" marks before your time is up. The scoring machine may count extraneous marks as wrong answers.

By using this overall approach, you are bound to achieve your best possible score.

II. The Elimination Strategy

Take advantage of being allowed to mark in the testing booklet. As you eliminate an incorrect answer choice from consideration, mark it out in your question booklet as follows:

(A̶)
?(B)
(C̶)
(D̶)
?(E)

Notice that some choices are marked with question marks, signifying that they may be possible answers. This technique will help you avoid reconsidering those choices you have already eliminated and will help you narrow down your possible answers.

These marks in your *testing booklet* need not be erased.

Part II: Analysis of Exam Areas

This section is designed to introduce you to each LSAT area by carefully reviewing the

1. Ability Tested
2. Basic Skills Necessary
3. Directions
4. Analysis of Directions
5. Suggested Approach with Sample Questions

This section features the PATTERNED PLAN OF ATTACK for each subject area and emphasizes important test-taking techniques and strategies and how to apply them to a variety of problem types.

INTRODUCTION TO WRITING THE ESSAY

Ability Tested

This section tests your ability to express your opinion clearly and logically in writing, adhering to the rules and conventions of standard written English.

Basic Skills Necessary

Repeated practice in responding to LSAT essay topics should enrich and improve the basic writing skills you already possess.

Directions

You are to plan and write a brief essay, given no more than thirty minutes. Recent LSAT topics present you with two candidates for a job or two items. The criteria for considering both candidates or items, along with a brief description of each candidate's qualifications or each item's qualities, are provided. You must write an argument for hiring *one* of the candidates or choosing one of the items. YOU MUST WRITE ON THE GIVEN TOPIC ONLY.

The quality of your writing is more important than either the quantity of writing or the point of view you adopt. Your skill in organization, mechanics, and usage is important, although it is expected that your essay will not be flawless because of the time pressure under which you write.

You will be given an essay booklet that consists of a sheet of paper approximately 8½" by 14", which contains about 60 5-inch lines upon which to write. Keep your writing within the lined area of your essay booklet. Write on every line, avoid wide margins, do not write any part of your essay on the back of the sheet, and write carefully and legibly. You should use a sheet of correct size for practice purposes.

Analysis

1. You must respond only to the given topic. Your response will require no special knowledge in any area but will draw from your general knowledge and background.

2. You may choose to argue for *either* candidate or item; there is no "right" or "wrong" choice. Careful, clear writing, no matter what position you take, is most important.

3. Allow some time at the beginning of the thirty-minute period to plan your argument and some time to proofread your work before time is called. The time you will have for actually writing the argument will be brief; therefore, you should expect your finished essay to be brief—probably not completely filling the space provided.

4. Neat, legible handwriting (or printing) is important. Your readers will be distracted from the quality of your response if it is hard to read.

Suggested Approach with Samples

Read the following description of Fez and Durango, candidates for promotion from associate professor to full professor at I.Q. University. *Then, in the space provided, write an argument for promoting either Fez or Durango.* Use the information in this description and assume that two general policies guide the I.Q.U. decisions on promotion:

1. Promotions are based on teaching effectiveness, professional growth, and service to the university.
2. The publication of scholarly books and articles is recognized as professional growth.

Fez won the university award for distinguished teaching during both of his first two years at I.Q.U. Student evaluations of his classroom effectiveness have been consistently high; many students rate him the best teacher they have ever had. At the request of his department chairperson, Fez served for one year on the busy and challenging Faculty Development Committee, helping to prepare a lengthy report evaluating the year's work. Since arriving at I.Q., he has served on a less busy but important university committee, the President's Advisory Group. He has published a long and well-reviewed article in the most prestigious scholarly journal in his field and just recently contracted with a major publisher to complete a book summarizing the important research conducted over the last ten years by his most distinguished colleagues.

Durango has published three major books based on his own research and controversial ideas. One of the books was a best-seller for twenty weeks. Durango has a remarkable talent for writing, manifest not only in his major books but also in the scores of articles he places in numerous scholarly journals. Because he is a controversial thinker and because of his generally abrasive personality, Durango is not popular with most students; however, a few very bright students have appreciated the refreshing quality of Durango's thought. Deeply concerned with the welfare of the university and curious about all the inner workings of the institution, Durango has volunteered over the years to serve on a number of university committees. However, his offer to serve has sometimes been refused by other committee members who have difficulty working with him.

1. Read and mark the relevant criteria. In this case, the criteria are *teaching effectiveness, professional growth,* and *service. Professional growth* consists of *scholarly publication.*

2. Read the descriptions of each candidate and chart their qualifications with reference to the criteria:

	Fez	*Durango*
teaching	award/high evals	abrasive/bright like him
growth	1 prestige article/ book in progress	3 books/controversial/ bestseller/many articles/
service	2 committees	volunteer/ hard to work with

3. Choose a candidate. Usually the two candidates' areas of greatest strength will differ. For instance, Fez is superior in the teaching area; Durango is superior in the professional growth area. Choose either candidate, but be prepared to argue that his *greatest strength* should be a *primary criterion.* For instance, if you choose Fez, you must propose that teaching excellence is the most important factor to consider and tell *why.* If you choose Durango, you must propose that *scholarly publication* is the most important factor and tell *why.*

4. Write a first paragraph which (1) emphasizes the significance of the candidate's strength(s) and (2) minimizes the significance of the candidate's weaknesses. The following *because-although-therefore* structure may be useful, but do be aware that you may wish to adjust this method to fit your own writing style and the specific requirements of the topic.

(greatest strength) should be our primary consideration *because* (explain). *Although* (other criteria) must be considered, achievement in (greatest strength) shows (explain). *Therefore,* we should hire (promote, select, etc.) (name of candidate) based on his (her) (achievement/strength).

Given the facts and criteria in this case, a *because-although-therefore* first paragraph might look as follows:

Excellence in teaching should be our primary consideration because if our professors are not effective in the classroom, they do not fulfill their responsibility—education. Although service and scholarship must also be considered, teaching effectiveness is the measure of success or failure "on the job." Therefore, we should promote Fez based on his teaching awards and evaluations.

An opening argument for Durango might proceed as follows:

Professional growth should be our primary consideration because without continuing research and publication, our faculty cannot contribute to the university's goal—increasing knowledge. Although teaching effectiveness and service must be considered, a candidate's scholarly writing best demonstrates strength and originality of intellect. Therefore, we should promote Durango based on his distinguished writing.

5. Write one "middle" paragraph that (1) reiterates and reemphasizes the candidate's strength(s) and (2) dismisses the weaknesses as unimportant *or* turns the weaknesses into strengths. Note that the middle section might appropriately contain two or three paragraphs, each of which would contain a logical division of your argument. Following is a single paragraph argument for Fez.

Consistent student praise is an unmistakable indication of fine teaching; the praise Fez has received, along with his awards, shows that he has improved the quality of our students' intellectual lives. His professional growth is also distinctive. Fez chose to patiently compose a long essay of high quality rather than to publish numerous brief articles in unimportant journals. He knows his subject well as is evident from his grasp of a wide range of important research, research which will appear in his forthcoming book. He has been willing to serve the university on committees when called but has not let excessive attention to service weaken the quality of his teaching.

6. *(Optional) Write a conclusion* that summarizes the result of choosing your candidate. This statement may be only one or two sentences long.

By promoting Fez, we affirm our dedication to good teaching and show that the welfare of our students is our first concern.

7. *Reread and edit your essay.* Neatly correct spelling, grammar, and usage errors. Do not make major changes at this time; such changes may weaken the legibility of your essay and require more time than you have remaining.

8. *Before you take the LSAT, practice.* Writing is a skill acquired almost exclusively through practice. Write on the topics provided in this book, under time constraints, and show your finished essays to a good, honest critic.

Sample LSAT Writing Topics

A. Read the following description of Wu and Bonilla, two candidates for conductor of the Pops Symphony Orchestra. *Then, in the space provided, write an argument for hiring either Wu or Bonilla.* The following facts are relevant to your decision:

1. The Pops Symphony conductor creates many of the orchestra's arrangements.
2. The hiring committee prefers a conductor with a national reputation and an entertaining stage personality.

   Wu has been the first violinist of the Pops Symphony for three years, assisting the conductor. Late during the last Pops season, when the conductor fell ill and was forced to retire, Wu took over the baton for the final week of concerts. His entertaining, almost acrobatic, style won over every audience, and his final concert was aired on nationwide television and received an enthusiastic response from critics and viewers. During the off season, Wu has dedicated himself to arranging traditional American favorites for performance at the Pops debut next Independence Day. His talent as an arranger remains to be heard.

Trained in Europe, Bonilla has been guest conductor of several distinguished symphony orchestras, and his spirited performances of serious classical music have made him an international celebrity. His recent arrangements of Broadway show tunes, which he presented as an encore to the classical program, were well received throughout Europe. Critics admire the dignity with which Bonilla conducts the orchestra during serious classical works and marvel at the energy and enthusiasm he exhibits at the podium during lighter, brighter pieces.

B. Read the following description of Matson and O'Hara, who are seeking the position of city manager of a small California coastal community. *Then, in the space provided, write an argument for appointing either Matson or O'Hara.* Use the information in the following descriptions and assume that two general concerns will guide the City Council in making the appointment:

1. The candidate's record as a supporter of a clean environment.
2. The candidate's ability to strengthen community support and volunteer service for a program of urban beautification projects.

Matson has been a resident of California for six years. While in California, she has served as an officer in Friends of Wildlife, an organization that helps protect rare animal species, and has contributed heavily to the Committee to Prevent Offshore Oil Drilling. Matson's father owns a small oil company in Texas. Matson left a senior position with that company, as public relations director, to move to the west coast. She just completed a year-long college course in landscape architecture, a subject that has always interested her. The course required that the students design three proposals for beautifying older sections of the city.

O'Hara is a native Californian who has lived in coastal communities all his life. Last year, while residing in Long Beach, he organized a large community protest against offshore drilling, managing to recruit a small staff, print and distribute hundreds of protest leaflets, and attract over 7,000 residents to a "Stop Oil" rally. He is a dues paying member of Save the Earth International, an environmental action group. For the last ten years, O'Hara has spent his vacation each year in the ghetto areas of Los Angeles, helping a community-sponsored group paint murals on the bare sides of tenement buildings. One of the murals has been highly praised by the senior art critic of the *Los Angeles Tribune*.

Previous Topic Type

The following topic type appeared on the LSAT until June of 1985 when the new-style topic was introduced.

The curriculum committee is meeting to evaluate the courses currently offered at your school. They have asked that students submit a description of their favorite course taken so far and some concrete reasons that the course is so valuable. The committee is more interested in learning the value of the course *content* than in receiving an evaluation of the instructor. Write a brief description and evaluation of your favorite course for this committee.

A PATTERNED PLAN OF ATTACK

Writing the Essay

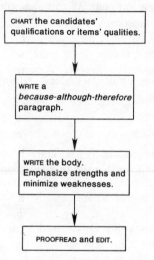

CHART the candidates' qualifications or items' qualities.

WRITE a *because-although-therefore* paragraph.

WRITE the body. Emphasize strengths and minimize weaknesses.

PROOFREAD and EDIT.

INTRODUCTION TO READING COMPREHENSION

Reading Comprehension lasts 35 minutes and typically contains four passages and 28 questions.

Ability Tested

This section tests your ability to understand, interpret, and analyze reading passages on a variety of topics.

Basic Skills Necessary

Students who have read widely and know how to read and mark a passage actively and efficiently tend to do well on this section.

Directions

Each passage in this group is followed by questions based on its content. After reading a passage, choose the best answer to each question and blacken the corresponding space on the answer sheet. Answer all questions following a passage on the basis of what is *stated* or *implied* in that passage. You may refer back to the passage.

Analysis

1. Answer all the questions for one passage before moving on to the next one. If you don't know the answer, take an educated guess. Don't leave blanks.
2. Use only the information given or implied in a passage. Do not consider outside information, even if it seems more accurate than the given information.

Suggested Approach with Short Sample Passage

1. Skim the questions first, marking words which give you a clue about what to look for when you read the passage.
2. Read the passage, marking main points, important conclusions, names, definitions, places, and numbers. But be careful not to overmark.

3. Answer the questions using only information from the passage, referring back to relevant parts of the passage whenever necessary.

• *Short Sample Passage*

St. Augustine was a contemporary of Jerome. After an early life of pleasure, he became interested in a philosophical religion called Manichaeism, a derivative of a Persian religion, in which the forces of good constantly struggle with those of evil. Augustine was eventually converted to Christianity by St. Ambrose of Milan. His *Confessions* was an autobiography that served as an inspiration to countless thousands who believed that virtue would ultimately win.

• *Sample Questions with Explanations*

1. St. Augustine's (conversion) to Christianity was probably influenced by
   (A) his confessional leanings
   (B) his contemporaries
   (C) the inadequacy of a Persian religion to address Western moral problems
   (D) his earlier interest in the dilemma of retaining virtue
   (E) the ravages of a life of pleasure

Having skimmed this question, you may have marked the portion of the passage which mentions Augustine's conversion and paid attention to the events (influences) leading to it. (A) requires speculating beyond the facts in the paragraph; there is also no evidence in the passage to support (C) or (E). (B) is too vague and general to be the best answer. (D) points toward Augustine's earlier interest in Manichaeism, and the last sentence suggests that Augustine's interest in retaining virtue continued through his Christian doctrine. Well supported as it is, (D) is the best answer.

2. From the information in the passage, we must conclude that Augustine was a
   (A) fair-weather optimist   (D) failed optimist
   (B) cockeyed optimist   (E) glib optimist
   (C) hardworking optimist

Skimming *this* question is not very helpful; it does not point specifically to any information in the passage, but the question does use *must,* pointing us toward a certain, rather than merely probable, conclusion. Questions of this sort usually assess your overall understanding of the meaning, style, tone, or point of view of the passage. In this case, you should recognize that Augustine is a serious person; therefore, more lighthearted terms like *fair-weather* (A), *cockeyed* (B), and *glib* (E) are definitely inappropriate. (D) contradicts Augustine's success as an "inspiration to countless thousands." (C) corresponds with his ongoing, hopeful struggle to retain virtue in the world; it is the best answer.

3. Judging from the reaction of thousands to Augustine's *Confessions,* we may conclude that much of his world at that time was in a state of

   (A) opulence   (D) reformation
   (B) misery   (E) sanctification
   (C) heresy

Having skimmed this question, you may have marked the last sentence of the passage as the place to look for the answer. That Augustine's readers were inspired implies that they *required inspiration,* that they were in some sort of uninspiring, or negative, situation. (A) and (E) must therefore be eliminated because they are positive terms. (D) is not necessarily a negative term and so is probably not the best answer. (C), although a negative term, does not describe a state of being which thirsts for inspiration. (B) does, and (B) therefore is the best choice.

Along with questions that ask for expressed or implied information and tone in the passage, such as the questions above, you will probably encounter questions that ask for (1) the primary purpose of the passage, (2) the main idea of the passage, and (3) the ways in which the author's ideas might be relevant to other situations.

A PATTERNED PLAN OF ATTACK

Reading Comprehension

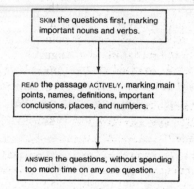

SKIM the questions first, marking important nouns and verbs.

READ the passage ACTIVELY, marking main points, names, definitions, important conclusions, places, and numbers.

ANSWER the questions, without spending too much time on any one question.

INTRODUCTION TO ANALYTICAL REASONING

The Analytical Reasoning section lasts 35 minutes and typically contains 24 questions.

Ability Tested

This section tests your ability to discern the relationships embodied in a set of conditions and to derive information from the conditions.

Basic Skills Necessary

The ability to organize abstract relationships in order to solve a "puzzle" is important here; students familiar with several ways of displaying such relationships are likely to do well.

Directions

You will be presented several sets of conditions. A group of questions follows each set of conditions. Choose the best answer to each question, drawing a rough diagram of the conditions when necessary.

Analysis

1. For this section, you are looking for the "correct" answer. Once you encounter a satisfactory answer, do not read and analyze other answer choices; mark as your answer choice the first correct answer you arrive at.

2. Displaying information—sketching diagrams and charts of the conditions is invaluable; not doing so significantly increases the difficulty of the problems.

SUGGESTED APPROACH WITH SAMPLES

Location Diagram (Simple)

Some Analytical Reasoning problems require that you organize information into a simple location diagram in order to more easily answer the questions. These problems deal with persons or items in certain positions, or places on maps, or objects in a line, etc. For instance:

• *Sample Problem*

1. Eight adults are seated around the perimeter of a square table.
2. An equal number of adults sits on each side.
3. A woman is always seated next to a man.
4. Half of the adults are women.
5. A woman is always seated between two men.

• *Questions*

1. Which of the following must be true?

    I. A man is always seated directly across from a woman.
   II. People of the same sex are sometimes seated directly across from each other.
  III. A man is seated between two women.

  (A) I only   (D) I and II
  (B) II only   (E) I and III
  (C) III only

2. Which of the original statements repeats information that may be inferred from previous statements?

  (A) 3   (D) none of the statements
  (B) 4   (E) cannot be determined
  (C) 5

3. If a man changes places with a woman to his right, which of the following must now be true?

    I. One side of the table will seat just men.
   II. One side of the table will seat just women.
  III. At least two sides of the table will seat a man and a woman.

  (A) I only   (D) I and II
  (B) II only   (E) I, II, and III
  (C) III only

• *Explanation*

To set up the diagram, simply draw the format (in this case a square table with two seats on each side) and fill in the seats accordingly. You should realize that there are two possible setups for this example:

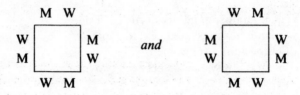

• *Answers*

Now that you've set up the location diagram, questions 1 and 3 are very easily answered simply by referring to your chart:

Question 1—Answer (E)

Question 2—Answer (D) None of the statements repeats information. Note that statement 5 eliminates this possible setup:

Question 3—Answer (C)

Location Diagram (Complex)

Some Analytical Reasoning questions require drawing a more complex "location diagram." These more complex diagrams may have variables within their structures or may even be incomplete— that is, you may not be able to completely fill in all of the diagram. For instance:

• *Sample Problem*

1. Six people are standing in a straight line to get tickets.
2. Each person is wearing a hat that is either blue, red, yellow, or green.
3. Each person is wearing a coat that is either red, brown, black, or blue.
4. The same colors may not be worn by people standing next to each other.
5. No one can wear a hat and coat that are the same color.
6. The third person in line is wearing a yellow hat and a brown coat.
7. The first person in line is wearing a red hat and a blue coat.
8. The sixth person in line is wearing a red coat.

• *Questions*

1. The second person in line must be wearing a
   - (A) yellow hat
   - (B) green hat
   - (C) red coat
   - (D) blue coat
   - (E) red hat

2. The second person in line must wear a coat that is
   - (A) red
   - (B) brown
   - (C) black
   - (D) blue
   - (E) either blue or red

3. If the fifth person wears a blue coat with a yellow hat, then the sixth person's hat must be

   I. red
   II. yellow
   III. green

   - (A) I
   - (B) II
   - (C) III
   - (D) I or III
   - (E) II or III

• *Explanation*

To set up the diagram, first draw the format as follows:

	1	2	3	4	5	6
Hat (R, Blu, Y, G)	R		Y			
Coat (R, Br, Bla, Blu)	Blu		Br			R

Then fill in the information given:

	1	2	3	4	5	6
Hat	R	G	Y			
Coat	Blu	Bla	Br			R

Nothing else can be completed, so at this point you should proceed to the questions.

• *Answers*

Question 1—Answer (B)
Question 2—Answer (C)
Question 3—Answer (C)

Notice that question 3 is an "if" question (it begins with the word *if*). Therefore, you may use your location diagram to help answer the question, but information given in this question should *not* be *permanently* entered into the diagram, as *it refers to this question only.*

Connection Chart

Another type of Analytical Reasoning problem requires the construction of a "connection chart." A connection chart is just a very simple diagram showing the relationship among numerous items. For instance:

• *Sample Problem*

Tom has been given six numbers (1, 2, 3, 4, 5, and 6) to make a decal.

The numbers are in different sizes and only certain sizes will look good together.

Tom will not combine sizes that will not look good together.

The 2 will not go well with the 6.

The 1 will go well with the 3 or the 4 but not with both together.

Tom must use the 1 or the 2, or both.

Tom may use only three symbols on the decal.

• Questions

1. If 3 and 6 are chosen, then

   I. 1 must be chosen
   II. 5 must be chosen
   III. 4 may be chosen

   (A) I only
   (B) II only
   (C) III only

   (D) two of these
   (E) three of these

2. If 4 and 5 are chosen, then
   (A) 3 may be chosen
   (B) 6 may be chosen
   (C) 2 must be chosen
   (D) 1 may be chosen
   (E) none of the above

3. If 6 is chosen, but 5 isn't chosen, which of the following may also be chosen?
   (A) 1 and 2
   (B) 1 and 4
   (C) 3 and 4

   (D) 2 and 3
   (E) 2 and 4

• Explanation

A connection diagram should be as simple as possible. For the sample question, the following diagram may be drawn:

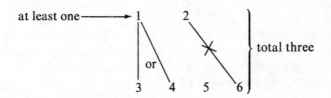

Notice that lines indicate which numbers will go together, but a line marked with an "x" indicates numbers which won't go well together. Also notice the positioning of the numbers (1 and 2 on top) shows that either or both from that row *must* be chosen.

• Answers

Now that the chart has been drawn, the questions are easily answered:

Question 1—Answer (A)
Question 2—Answer (D)
Question 3—Answer (B)

Elimination Chart

One type of Analytical Reasoning problem presents information which excludes or eliminates other possibilities. For instance, four people receiving four *different* grades or five animals belonging to five *different* owners—as soon as one item is placed, it narrows the placement of the other items.

• Sample Problem

1. Two men (Ben and Arnold) and two women (Lydia and Dolly) have four different professions: dancer, magician, violinist, and salesperson.
2. Ben is not the dancer.
3. The violinist is a woman.
4. The dancer is not a woman.
5. Dolly is the magician.

• Questions

1. Lydia is the
   (A) magician
   (B) dancer
   (C) violinist
   (D) salesperson
   (E) cannot be determined

2. If the two men switch professions, then

    I. Arnold will be the salesperson
   II. Arnold will be the dancer
  III. Ben will be the dancer

(A) I only   (D) I and II
(B) II only   (E) I and III
(C) III only

• *Explanation*

Set up your diagram; realize that as soon as an item is placed, you may then eliminate its possible placement anywhere else in the grid. Note that the grid and those following are presented very formally. In many cases you can arrive at the correct answer by using variations of these techniques in a less formal, simpler diagram or, in some cases, even mentally. Also, notice that you should also mark what you know is *not* true. For instance, first set up your diagram as follows:

	Magician	Violinist	Dancer	Salesperson
Ben				
Arnold				
Lydia				
Dolly				

Now notice that statement 2 allows you to eliminate Ben as the dancer:

	Magician	Violinist	Dancer	Salesperson
Ben			X	
Arnold				
Lydia				
Dolly				

Statement 3 eliminates either of the men from being the violinist:

	Magician	Violinist	Dancer	Salesperson
Ben		X	X	
Arnold		X		
Lydia				
Dolly				

Statement 4 tells you the dancer is not a woman:

	Magician	Violinist	Dancer	Salesperson
Ben		X	X	
Arnold		X		
Lydia			X	
Dolly			X	

Thus, you now know that the dancer *must* be Arnold. You should now eliminate magician and salesperson as possibilities for Arnold:

	Magician	Violinist	Dancer	Salesperson
Ben		X	X	
Arnold	X	X	✓	X
Lydia			X	
Dolly			X	

Statement 5 says that Dolly is the magician:

	Magician	Violinist	Dancer	Salesperson
Ben	X	X	X	
Arnold	X	X	✓	X
Lydia	X		X	
Dolly	✓	X	X	X

You can now see that Ben must be the salesperson, and Lydia must therefore be the violinist.

• *Answers*

Question 1—Answer (C)
Question 2—Answer (E)

Information Display

Some Analytical Reasoning problems won't fit into a neat diagram. Therefore, it may be helpful to simply list or display the information gathered from the conditions in as simple a way as possible. For instance:

• *Sample Problem*

In a litter of six puppies, three have floppy ears.
Two of the puppies are brown.
Five of the puppies are female.

• *Questions*

1. Which of the following must be true?

    I. At least two of the females have floppy ears.
    II. Three of the females have floppy ears.
    III. One of the brown puppies has floppy ears.

    (A) I only   (D) I and II
    (B) II only   (E) I, II, and III
    (C) III only

2. Which of the following must be true?
    (A) Two of the females are brown.
    (B) All of the females have floppy ears.
    (C) All of the brown puppies are females.
    (D) One of the females is brown with floppy ears.
    (E) One of the females is brown.

• *Explanation*

This particular problem does not fit into either a location, a connection, or an elimination diagram. But it may be helpful to display the facts in a simple diagram:

6 Puppies

Ears:	3 floppy	3 not floppy
Color:	2 brown	4 not brown
Sex:	5 females	1 male

• *Answers*

Question 1—Answer (A). Since five of the puppies are female, the sixth puppy (male) could have floppy ears, which would leave two of the females to have floppy ears.

Question 2—Answer (E). Since five of the six puppies are female, and since there are two brown puppies, at least one female must be brown.

A PATTERNED PLAN OF ATTACK

Analytical Reasoning

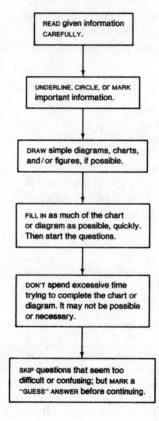

INTRODUCTION TO DISPUTE CHARACTERIZATION

The Dispute Characterization section (previously called Evaluation of Facts) lasts 35 minutes and typically contains 35 to 40 questions.

Ability Tested

This section tests your ability both to read with understanding and precision and to reason accurately.

Basic Skills Necessary

Important skills for this section are the ability to pinpoint key issues from the facts and to distinguish between important differences stated in the rules.

Directions

You are presented with a narrative of facts, a dispute, and two rules. Sometimes the rules are conflicting, sometimes not; but in any case each rule should be considered independent of the other. Questions follow each set of rules. You are to classify each question according to the following choices:

(A) A relevant question whose answer requires a choice between the rules.

(B) A relevant question whose answer does not require a choice between the rules but requires additional facts or rules.

(C) A relevant question that is readily answerable from the facts or rules or both.

(D) An irrelevant question or one whose answer bears only remotely on the outcome of the dispute.

Analysis

1. The first determination is whether the question is relevant. If it is not relevant to the dispute, mark (D). If it is relevant, eliminate (D) and continue to . . .

2. Determine if the question is readily answerable from the facts and/or rules. That is, if the answer to this question immediately

jumps out at you, then choose (C). If you cannot choose (C), then continue on to . . .
3. Determine if the question requires a choice *between* the rules. That is, do the rules conflict such that each one would provide a different answer to the question and there is no reason to apply one rule over the other? If such a choice is necessary, then choose (A). If even a choice between the rules will not provide an answer, then the only answer left is (B), meaning that additional facts or rules are necessary to reach a decisive answer.

NOTE:

1. No legal knowledge or specialized information is necessary for this section. Work only from the information given.
2. One rule does not automatically take precedence over the other.
3. Evaluate each question independently of the other questions.

Suggested Approach with Samples

• *Sample Set*

Facts: Almost every evening during summer vacation, the neighborhood children played street football in front of the Beddoes' house. Julia and Stewart Beddoe would often taunt their playmate, Peter Griswold, to unnerve him as he tried to pass the football. The Beddoe children had been warned several times by their own parents and by Peter's to leave Peter alone and play more fairly. One evening, while Peter was trying to pass the football, Julia Beddoe tossed a pebble into his eye. Peter's pass went awry and broke the picture window in the Beddoes' front room. Peter was taken to the hospital emergency room where his injury was diagnosed as a scratched cornea. The physician placed an eyepatch over the damaged eye and prescribed a month's supply of pain-killing medication.

Dispute: Peter's parents sued the Beddoes for damages caused by their child Julia. The Beddoes contested.

Rule I: Parents are liable for any damages or injuries to another caused by the actions of their children.

Rule II: Children under eight years of age, or their parents, are not
liable for damages or injuries that the children may have
caused.

Questions:

1. Was Julia over seven years of age?
2. Was Peter a good passer?
3. If Julia is ten years old, who will win the suit?
4. If Julia is seven years old, who will win the suit?
5. Was Peter injured?
6. If Peter's injury was not caused by the pebble, will the Beddoes
   win the suit?

• *Approach*

1. Read actively, marking key words or phrases in the facts and
   dispute. Note the markings in the facts and dispute below; your
   markings may include different information.

   Facts: Almost every evening during summer vacation, the neighborhood children played street football in front of the
   Beddoes' house. Julia and Stewart Beddoe would often
   taunt their playmate, Peter Griswold, to unnerve him as he
   tried to pass the football. The Beddoe children had been
   warned several times by their own parents and by Peter's
   to leave Peter alone and play more fairly. One evening,
   while Peter was trying to pass the football, Julia Beddoe
   tossed a pebble into his eye. Peter's pass went awry and
   broke the picture window in the Beddoes' front room.
   Peter was taken to the hospital emergency room where his
   injury was diagnosed as a scratched cornea. The physician
   placed an eyepatch over the damaged eye and prescribed a
   month's supply of pain-killing medication.

   Dispute: Peter's parents sued the Beddoes for damages caused by
   their child. The Beddoes contested.

2. Mark and note the difference between the rules. Look for the
   words that limit, expand, or detail the rules. Watchwords are often

words like: *only, must, if, never, always, although, without, except, at least,* etc. Knowing the similarities among and differences between the rules is essential. Notice the way the following rules have been marked:

Rule I: (Parents are liable) for any damages or injuries to another caused by the actions of their children.

Rule II: Children (under eight years of age,) or their parents, (are not liable) for damages or injuries that the children may have caused.

3. In classifying the questions, always check first to see if the question is relevant. If it is, see if an answer *jumps* out at you.

4. Follow the pattern if nothing jumps; work through each possible answer systematically but quickly.

5. Remember these distinctions:

(A) To choose (A), you must get two different answers depending upon which rule you choose, *and* there must be no reason to choose one particular rule over the other. Simple factual questions referring to *how* or *when* something happened, or what the value of an object is, will usually NOT be answer (A).

(B) To choose (B), you must need additional facts or rules to answer the question. Often the definition of a key word or phrase in the rules will be the basis of a question requiring a (B) answer.

(C) To choose (C), you must be able to answer the question, getting only one answer. This will happen because you are led to one rule or one rule is eliminated from consideration. Sometimes here *both* rules can be applied and will give the same answer.

(D) To choose (D), the question must be irrelevant or only very remotely bear on the dispute. The question may be an issue that is not considered or covered by the rules and is not targeted at the dispute.

• *Answers and Explanations to Questions*

1. Was Julia over seven years of age?

   (B) This is a relevant question because her age will determine which rule to choose in deciding the dispute. Since we do not know her age, we need additional facts.

2. Was Peter a good passer?

   (D) Whether or not Peter is a good passer is irrelevant and has no bearing on the rules or the dispute.

3. If Julia is ten years old, who will win the suit?

   (C) If Julia is ten years old, then both rules lead to the same answer: The Beddoes will lose the suit.

4. If Julia is seven years old, who will win the suit?

   (A) If Julia is seven years old, then each rule gives a different answer. Rule I—the Beddoes will lose. Rule II—the Beddoes will win. There is no reason to choose one rule over the other (remember, neither rule takes precedence). Therefore a choice is necessary.

5. Was Peter injured?

   (C) This is a relevant question which may be answered from the facts. Yes, he was injured (scratched cornea).

6. If Peter's injury was not caused by the pebble, will the Beddoes win the suit?

   (B) This question is relevant to the dispute but cannot be answered by the rules. More information about the injury or more rules are necessary in order to answer the question.

A PATTERNED PLAN OF ATTACK

Dispute Characterization

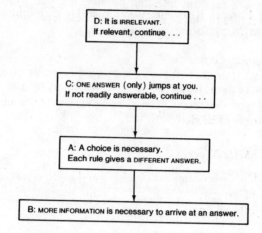

D: It is IRRELEVANT.
If relevant, continue . . .

C: ONE ANSWER (only) jumps at you.
If not readily answerable, continue . . .

A: A choice is necessary.
Each rule gives a DIFFERENT ANSWER.

B: MORE INFORMATION is necessary to arrive at an answer.

INTRODUCTION TO LOGICAL REASONING

The Logical Reasoning section lasts 35 minutes and typically contains 26 questions.

Ability Tested

This section tests your ability to analyze and evaluate short passages or statements drawn from a variety of sources and presented in a variety of modes.

Basic Skills Necessary

Students who can read critically and understand major issues and points of view tend to do well in this section. Ability to eliminate irrelevant and unimportant issues is also important.

Directions

You will be presented with brief passages or statements and will be required to evaluate their reasoning. In each case, select the best answer choice, even though more than one choice may present a possible answer. Choices which are unreasonable or incompatible with common-sense standards should be eliminated.

Analysis

1. Use only information given or implied in a passage. Do not consider outside information, even if it seems more accurate than the given information.
2. Note the stress on choosing the BEST answer; the testmakers strongly imply that there may be more than one good answer.
3. No special expertise in logic is necessary; do not arrive at your answer choice through the use of formal logical principles; rely on common sense.

Suggested Approach with Samples

1. In most cases, the question will have the following structure: reading passage—question—multiple choices. Always read the

41

question first so that you have an idea of what to look for when you read the passage.

Reading Passage: Whatever else might be said about American elections, they are already quite unlike Soviet elections in that Americans make choices. And one choice they can make in this free country is to stay home.

Question: What is the author's point in the above passage?

Multiple Choices:
(A) Americans who do decide to vote make more choices than those who do not.
(B) American elections embody many negative aspects, most of which are not embodied by Soviet elections.
(C) Choosing not to vote is the prerogative of a free citizen.
(D) All citizens vote in every Soviet election.
(E) Most American voters are not well informed enough to vote wisely.

Prereading the question allows you to read the passage with a *focus*. In this case, you are looking for the author's point; recognizing the concluding sentence as the author's point is valuable here.

2. Keep the question in mind when reading a passage, and also note the major issue and supporting evidence in the passage. Ask yourself, what is this passage, in general, about? The answer relative to the passage above is "free choice." Evidence supporting the issue of free choice is (1) the fact that Americans make choices when they vote and (2) the fact that Americans may make the choice not to vote.

3. When considering the multiple choices, immediately eliminate those items which are (1) irrelevant to the question and/or the major issue of the passage and (2) not at all addressed by the passage. Consider the passage above. The author's point is necessarily connected with the major issue of the passage—in this case, free choice. The author stresses the free choice *not to vote,* by way

of making the point. You may eliminate all choices which do not address the free choice not to vote: (A) is irrelevant because it addresses the number of choices rather than the freedom of choice; (B) raises issues scarcely addressed in the passage—that is, the negative aspects of elections. (D) doesn't address the issue of choosing not to vote; though it notes that all Soviet citizens must vote, it neglects the main point—that Americans don't have to; (E) is irrelevant to the issue of free choice, stressing instead voter information. The best choice is (C), which addresses the major issue, free choice, and also the author's specific point, the free choice not to vote.

4. A question may require you to evaluate tone:

Interviewer: How do you like the clean, fresh taste of new MaxoShine Toothbrightener?

Interviewee: My dentist tells me that no toothpaste will affect the natural color of my teeth.

In the above exchange, the interviewer's question implies which of the following attitudes toward MaxoShine?
(A) sincere curiosity
(B) unqualified enthusiasm
(C) unabashed ignorance
(D) scientific objectivity
(E) disguised dislike

The question asks about the interviewer's attitude, and questions like this which ask you to define the author's *stance* in one way or another are often answerable through noting the tone. In order to detect tone, do this: (1) When you read the passage in question, do so *actively,* trying to suit the "personality" of the words to the purpose or structure of the passage. In the passage above, the purpose of the interviewer is to advocate the product, and the structure of the passage is a dialogue. (2) When you read, imagine the way in which such an interviewer might deliver the question and try to mentally approximate the tone of a conversational exchange.

Note that the tone of the interviewer is extremely positive, and that certain modifiers within the interviewer's question stress that positive attitude (modifiers such as *clean, fresh, new*). Noting this tone leads you to eliminate choices which indicate a neutral or negative attitude and to realize that the only answer choice coincident with the interviewer's positive tone is (B).

A question about the interviewee might lead you to consider the negative attitude expressed there and also to note that the interviewee does not really answer the question asked.

5. Recognizing the "type" of question asked will help to lead you to a correct answer. Questions will commonly ask you to (1) identify the author's main point, (2) identify the author's underlying assumptions, (3) identify information which strengthens the author's conclusion, (4) identify flaws in the argument or conclusion, or characteristics which weaken it.

Identifying the Author's Main Point

Identifying the main issue, as described above, will help you to answer this type of question.

Identifying the Author's Underlying Assumptions

The assumption of the author is that which motivates his or her argument. For instance, an argument in favor of increased government spending *assumes* that present government spending is too low. An example:

United States dependence on foreign oil has tended to overshadow the beneficial effects of gasoline-powered machines on our society. More than ever before, the American automobile allows us to enjoy the many pleasures this country offers.

The argument above is based upon which of the following assumptions?

I. Many American pleasures cannot be walked to.
II. The automobile is a significant gasoline-powered machine.
III. U.S. dependence on foreign oil is beneficial.

(A) I only   (D) I and II
(B) II only   (E) I and III
(C) III only

Answer and Explanation: (D) I and II. I is true (eliminate B and C because neither contains I). II is true (eliminate A and E). Choose (D) because it's the only choice left. Notice that by working from the roman numerals in this way, you did not need to spend time considering III.

Identifying Information Which Strengthens the Author's Argument or Conclusion

Focus on the *conclusion,* note the supporting evidence given, and look for an answer choice which supplies additional support specifically appropriate to the conclusion.

Identifying Information Which Weakens the Author's Argument or Conclusion

Look for answer choices which contradict or call into question the supporting evidence. An example:

United States dependence on foreign oil has tended to over-shadow the beneficial effects of gasoline-powered machines on our society. More than ever before, the American automobile allows us to enjoy the many pleasures this country offers.

This argument would be weakened by pointing out that

   I. smog generated by automobiles is not a pleasure
  II. at the turn of the century, Americans rarely ventured far from home
 III. inflation helped by rising oil prices has made many automobiles virtually unaffordable

(A) I and III   (D) I and II
(B) II and III   (E) I, II, and III
(C) II only

Answer and Explanation: (A) I and III. This problem also combines roman numeral choices and letter choices; it's a kind of *multiple-multiple choice.* Work from the numeral choices, asking yourself whether each is *true* or *false.* Statement I is true—it would weaken the argument for pleasure. Eliminate (B) and (C) because they do not contain I. II is false—it would *not* weaken the argument for driving as a modern pleasure. Eliminate (D) and (E) because both contain II. III is true—it would weaken the argument for automobiles as a source of pleasure. Choose (A), the only remaining possibility.

The strategies reviewed in this introduction are further explained and illustrated in the answers and explanations which follow each practice test. To summarize:

1. Preread questions when appropriate.
2. Focus on the major issue and supporting evidence.
3. Eliminate answer choices which are irrelevant.
4. Note the tone of the passage.
5. Note the "type" of question asked.

A PATTERNED PLAN OF ATTACK

Logical Reasoning

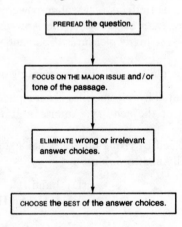

Part III: Practice-Review-Analyze-Practice

Two Full-Length Practice Tests

This section contains two full-length practice simulation LSATs. The practice tests are followed by complete answers, explanations, and analysis techniques. The format, levels of difficulty, question structure, and number of questions are similar to those on the actual LSAT. The actual LSAT is copyrighted and may not be duplicated, and these questions are not taken directly from the actual tests.

When taking these exams, try to simulate the test conditions by following the time allotments carefully.

PRACTICE TEST 1

Writing Essay—30 Minutes
Section I: Reading Comprehension—35 Minutes; 27 Questions
Section II: Analytical Reasoning—35 Minutes; 26 Questions
Section III: Dispute Characterization—35 Minutes; 40 Questions
Section IV: Logical Reasoning—35 Minutes; 26 Questions
Section V: Analytical Reasoning—35 Minutes; 26 Questions
Section VI: Reading Comprehension—35 Minutes; 28 Questions

ANSWER SHEET FOR PRACTICE TEST 1
(Remove This Sheet and Use It to Mark Your Answers)

SECTION I   SECTION II   SECTION III

SECTION I

1 Ⓐ Ⓑ Ⓒ Ⓓ Ⓔ
2 Ⓐ Ⓑ Ⓒ Ⓓ Ⓔ
3 Ⓐ Ⓑ Ⓒ Ⓓ Ⓔ
4 Ⓐ Ⓑ Ⓒ Ⓓ Ⓔ
5 Ⓐ Ⓑ Ⓒ Ⓓ Ⓔ
6 Ⓐ Ⓑ Ⓒ Ⓓ Ⓔ
7 Ⓐ Ⓑ Ⓒ Ⓓ Ⓔ
8 Ⓐ Ⓑ Ⓒ Ⓓ Ⓔ
9 Ⓐ Ⓑ Ⓒ Ⓓ Ⓔ
10 Ⓐ Ⓑ Ⓒ Ⓓ Ⓔ
11 Ⓐ Ⓑ Ⓒ Ⓓ Ⓔ
12 Ⓐ Ⓑ Ⓒ Ⓓ Ⓔ
13 Ⓐ Ⓑ Ⓒ Ⓓ Ⓔ
14 Ⓐ Ⓑ Ⓒ Ⓓ Ⓔ
15 Ⓐ Ⓑ Ⓒ Ⓓ Ⓔ
16 Ⓐ Ⓑ Ⓒ Ⓓ Ⓔ
17 Ⓐ Ⓑ Ⓒ Ⓓ Ⓔ
18 Ⓐ Ⓑ Ⓒ Ⓓ Ⓔ
19 Ⓐ Ⓑ Ⓒ Ⓓ Ⓔ
20 Ⓐ Ⓑ Ⓒ Ⓓ Ⓔ
21 Ⓐ Ⓑ Ⓒ Ⓓ Ⓔ
22 Ⓐ Ⓑ Ⓒ Ⓓ Ⓔ
23 Ⓐ Ⓑ Ⓒ Ⓓ Ⓔ
24 Ⓐ Ⓑ Ⓒ Ⓓ Ⓔ
25 Ⓐ Ⓑ Ⓒ Ⓓ Ⓔ
26 Ⓐ Ⓑ Ⓒ Ⓓ Ⓔ
27 Ⓐ Ⓑ Ⓒ Ⓓ Ⓔ

SECTION II

1 Ⓐ Ⓑ Ⓒ Ⓓ Ⓔ
2 Ⓐ Ⓑ Ⓒ Ⓓ Ⓔ
3 Ⓐ Ⓑ Ⓒ Ⓓ Ⓔ
4 Ⓐ Ⓑ Ⓒ Ⓓ Ⓔ
5 Ⓐ Ⓑ Ⓒ Ⓓ Ⓔ
6 Ⓐ Ⓑ Ⓒ Ⓓ Ⓔ
7 Ⓐ Ⓑ Ⓒ Ⓓ Ⓔ
8 Ⓐ Ⓑ Ⓒ Ⓓ Ⓔ
9 Ⓐ Ⓑ Ⓒ Ⓓ Ⓔ
10 Ⓐ Ⓑ Ⓒ Ⓓ Ⓔ
11 Ⓐ Ⓑ Ⓒ Ⓓ Ⓔ
12 Ⓐ Ⓑ Ⓒ Ⓓ Ⓔ
13 Ⓐ Ⓑ Ⓒ Ⓓ Ⓔ
14 Ⓐ Ⓑ Ⓒ Ⓓ Ⓔ
15 Ⓐ Ⓑ Ⓒ Ⓓ Ⓔ
16 Ⓐ Ⓑ Ⓒ Ⓓ Ⓔ
17 Ⓐ Ⓑ Ⓒ Ⓓ Ⓔ
18 Ⓐ Ⓑ Ⓒ Ⓓ Ⓔ
19 Ⓐ Ⓑ Ⓒ Ⓓ Ⓔ
20 Ⓐ Ⓑ Ⓒ Ⓓ Ⓔ
21 Ⓐ Ⓑ Ⓒ Ⓓ Ⓔ
22 Ⓐ Ⓑ Ⓒ Ⓓ Ⓔ
23 Ⓐ Ⓑ Ⓒ Ⓓ Ⓔ
24 Ⓐ Ⓑ Ⓒ Ⓓ Ⓔ
25 Ⓐ Ⓑ Ⓒ Ⓓ Ⓔ
26 Ⓐ Ⓑ Ⓒ Ⓓ Ⓔ

SECTION III

1 Ⓐ Ⓑ Ⓒ Ⓓ Ⓔ
2 Ⓐ Ⓑ Ⓒ Ⓓ Ⓔ
3 Ⓐ Ⓑ Ⓒ Ⓓ Ⓔ
4 Ⓐ Ⓑ Ⓒ Ⓓ Ⓔ
5 Ⓐ Ⓑ Ⓒ Ⓓ Ⓔ
6 Ⓐ Ⓑ Ⓒ Ⓓ Ⓔ
7 Ⓐ Ⓑ Ⓒ Ⓓ Ⓔ
8 Ⓐ Ⓑ Ⓒ Ⓓ Ⓔ
9 Ⓐ Ⓑ Ⓒ Ⓓ Ⓔ
10 Ⓐ Ⓑ Ⓒ Ⓓ Ⓔ
11 Ⓐ Ⓑ Ⓒ Ⓓ Ⓔ
12 Ⓐ Ⓑ Ⓒ Ⓓ Ⓔ
13 Ⓐ Ⓑ Ⓒ Ⓓ Ⓔ
14 Ⓐ Ⓑ Ⓒ Ⓓ Ⓔ
15 Ⓐ Ⓑ Ⓒ Ⓓ Ⓔ
16 Ⓐ Ⓑ Ⓒ Ⓓ Ⓔ
17 Ⓐ Ⓑ Ⓒ Ⓓ Ⓔ
18 Ⓐ Ⓑ Ⓒ Ⓓ Ⓔ
19 Ⓐ Ⓑ Ⓒ Ⓓ Ⓔ
20 Ⓐ Ⓑ Ⓒ Ⓓ Ⓔ
21 Ⓐ Ⓑ Ⓒ Ⓓ Ⓔ
22 Ⓐ Ⓑ Ⓒ Ⓓ Ⓔ
23 Ⓐ Ⓑ Ⓒ Ⓓ Ⓔ
24 Ⓐ Ⓑ Ⓒ Ⓓ Ⓔ
25 Ⓐ Ⓑ Ⓒ Ⓓ Ⓔ
26 Ⓐ Ⓑ Ⓒ Ⓓ Ⓔ
27 Ⓐ Ⓑ Ⓒ Ⓓ Ⓔ
28 Ⓐ Ⓑ Ⓒ Ⓓ Ⓔ
29 Ⓐ Ⓑ Ⓒ Ⓓ Ⓔ
30 Ⓐ Ⓑ Ⓒ Ⓓ Ⓔ

31 Ⓐ Ⓑ Ⓒ Ⓓ Ⓔ
32 Ⓐ Ⓑ Ⓒ Ⓓ Ⓔ
33 Ⓐ Ⓑ Ⓒ Ⓓ Ⓔ
34 Ⓐ Ⓑ Ⓒ Ⓓ Ⓔ
35 Ⓐ Ⓑ Ⓒ Ⓓ Ⓔ
36 Ⓐ Ⓑ Ⓒ Ⓓ Ⓔ
37 Ⓐ Ⓑ Ⓒ Ⓓ Ⓔ
38 Ⓐ Ⓑ Ⓒ Ⓓ Ⓔ
39 Ⓐ Ⓑ Ⓒ Ⓓ Ⓔ
40 Ⓐ Ⓑ Ⓒ Ⓓ Ⓔ

ANSWER SHEET FOR PRACTICE TEST 1
(Remove This Sheet and Use It to Mark Your Answers)

SECTION IV SECTION V SECTION VI

SECTION IV	SECTION V	SECTION VI
1 Ⓐ Ⓑ Ⓒ Ⓓ Ⓔ	1 Ⓐ Ⓑ Ⓒ Ⓓ Ⓔ	1 Ⓐ Ⓑ Ⓒ Ⓓ Ⓔ
2 Ⓐ Ⓑ Ⓒ Ⓓ Ⓔ	2 Ⓐ Ⓑ Ⓒ Ⓓ Ⓔ	2 Ⓐ Ⓑ Ⓒ Ⓓ Ⓔ
3 Ⓐ Ⓑ Ⓒ Ⓓ Ⓔ	3 Ⓐ Ⓑ Ⓒ Ⓓ Ⓔ	3 Ⓐ Ⓑ Ⓒ Ⓓ Ⓔ
4 Ⓐ Ⓑ Ⓒ Ⓓ Ⓔ	4 Ⓐ Ⓑ Ⓒ Ⓓ Ⓔ	4 Ⓐ Ⓑ Ⓒ Ⓓ Ⓔ
5 Ⓐ Ⓑ Ⓒ Ⓓ Ⓔ	5 Ⓐ Ⓑ Ⓒ Ⓓ Ⓔ	5 Ⓐ Ⓑ Ⓒ Ⓓ Ⓔ
6 Ⓐ Ⓑ Ⓒ Ⓓ Ⓔ	6 Ⓐ Ⓑ Ⓒ Ⓓ Ⓔ	6 Ⓐ Ⓑ Ⓒ Ⓓ Ⓔ
7 Ⓐ Ⓑ Ⓒ Ⓓ Ⓔ	7 Ⓐ Ⓑ Ⓒ Ⓓ Ⓔ	7 Ⓐ Ⓑ Ⓒ Ⓓ Ⓔ
8 Ⓐ Ⓑ Ⓒ Ⓓ Ⓔ	8 Ⓐ Ⓑ Ⓒ Ⓓ Ⓔ	8 Ⓐ Ⓑ Ⓒ Ⓓ Ⓔ
9 Ⓐ Ⓑ Ⓒ Ⓓ Ⓔ	9 Ⓐ Ⓑ Ⓒ Ⓓ Ⓔ	9 Ⓐ Ⓑ Ⓒ Ⓓ Ⓔ
10 Ⓐ Ⓑ Ⓒ Ⓓ Ⓔ	10 Ⓐ Ⓑ Ⓒ Ⓓ Ⓔ	10 Ⓐ Ⓑ Ⓒ Ⓓ Ⓔ
11 Ⓐ Ⓑ Ⓒ Ⓓ Ⓔ	11 Ⓐ Ⓑ Ⓒ Ⓓ Ⓔ	11 Ⓐ Ⓑ Ⓒ Ⓓ Ⓔ
12 Ⓐ Ⓑ Ⓒ Ⓓ Ⓔ	12 Ⓐ Ⓑ Ⓒ Ⓓ Ⓔ	12 Ⓐ Ⓑ Ⓒ Ⓓ Ⓔ
13 Ⓐ Ⓑ Ⓒ Ⓓ Ⓔ	13 Ⓐ Ⓑ Ⓒ Ⓓ Ⓔ	13 Ⓐ Ⓑ Ⓒ Ⓓ Ⓔ
14 Ⓐ Ⓑ Ⓒ Ⓓ Ⓔ	14 Ⓐ Ⓑ Ⓒ Ⓓ Ⓔ	14 Ⓐ Ⓑ Ⓒ Ⓓ Ⓔ
15 Ⓐ Ⓑ Ⓒ Ⓓ Ⓔ	15 Ⓐ Ⓑ Ⓒ Ⓓ Ⓔ	15 Ⓐ Ⓑ Ⓒ Ⓓ Ⓔ
16 Ⓐ Ⓑ Ⓒ Ⓓ Ⓔ	16 Ⓐ Ⓑ Ⓒ Ⓓ Ⓔ	16 Ⓐ Ⓑ Ⓒ Ⓓ Ⓔ
17 Ⓐ Ⓑ Ⓒ Ⓓ Ⓔ	17 Ⓐ Ⓑ Ⓒ Ⓓ Ⓔ	17 Ⓐ Ⓑ Ⓒ Ⓓ Ⓔ
18 Ⓐ Ⓑ Ⓒ Ⓓ Ⓔ	18 Ⓐ Ⓑ Ⓒ Ⓓ Ⓔ	18 Ⓐ Ⓑ Ⓒ Ⓓ Ⓔ
19 Ⓐ Ⓑ Ⓒ Ⓓ Ⓔ	19 Ⓐ Ⓑ Ⓒ Ⓓ Ⓔ	19 Ⓐ Ⓑ Ⓒ Ⓓ Ⓔ
20 Ⓐ Ⓑ Ⓒ Ⓓ Ⓔ	20 Ⓐ Ⓑ Ⓒ Ⓓ Ⓔ	20 Ⓐ Ⓑ Ⓒ Ⓓ Ⓔ
21 Ⓐ Ⓑ Ⓒ Ⓓ Ⓔ	21 Ⓐ Ⓑ Ⓒ Ⓓ Ⓔ	21 Ⓐ Ⓑ Ⓒ Ⓓ Ⓔ
22 Ⓐ Ⓑ Ⓒ Ⓓ Ⓔ	22 Ⓐ Ⓑ Ⓒ Ⓓ Ⓔ	22 Ⓐ Ⓑ Ⓒ Ⓓ Ⓔ
23 Ⓐ Ⓑ Ⓒ Ⓓ Ⓔ	23 Ⓐ Ⓑ Ⓒ Ⓓ Ⓔ	23 Ⓐ Ⓑ Ⓒ Ⓓ Ⓔ
24 Ⓐ Ⓑ Ⓒ Ⓓ Ⓔ	24 Ⓐ Ⓑ Ⓒ Ⓓ Ⓔ	24 Ⓐ Ⓑ Ⓒ Ⓓ Ⓔ
25 Ⓐ Ⓑ Ⓒ Ⓓ Ⓔ	25 Ⓐ Ⓑ Ⓒ Ⓓ Ⓔ	25 Ⓐ Ⓑ Ⓒ Ⓓ Ⓔ
26 Ⓐ Ⓑ Ⓒ Ⓓ Ⓔ	26 Ⓐ Ⓑ Ⓒ Ⓓ Ⓔ	26 Ⓐ Ⓑ Ⓒ Ⓓ Ⓔ
		27 Ⓐ Ⓑ Ⓒ Ⓓ Ⓔ
		28 Ⓐ Ⓑ Ⓒ Ⓓ Ⓔ

-- CUT HERE

WRITING ESSAY

Time: 30 Minutes

DIRECTIONS

You are to complete a brief essay on the given topic. You may take no more than 30 minutes to plan and write your essay. After reading the topics carefully, you should probably spend a few minutes planning and organizing your response. YOU MAY NOT WRITE ON A TOPIC OTHER THAN THE GIVEN TOPIC.

The quality of your writing is more important than either the quantity of writing or the point of view you adopt. Your skill in organization, mechanics, and usage is important, although it is expected that your essay will not be flawless because of the time pressure under which you write.

Keep your writing within the lined area of your essay booklet. Write on every line, avoid wide margins, and write carefully and legibly.

Essay Topic

Read the following descriptions of Mariano and Matisse, two applicants for the position of banquet manager at the St. Germaine hotel. *Then, in the space provided, write an argument for hiring either Mariano or Matisse.* The following criteria are relevant to your decision:

1. The banquet manager must plan parties for a variety of ethnic, religious, community, and business groups.
2. The banquet manager coordinates all the elements of each party (food, music, liquor, special presentations, etc.) and serves as master of ceremonies at the guests' request.

Mariano has been a popular independent bandleader and entertainer in the local area for twenty years. He and his musicians have performed at hundreds of wedding receptions, bar mitzvahs, anniversary celebrations, and holiday parties. Mariano prides himself on the scope of his musical knowledge: no guest has ever requested a song that he could not play. Mariano has worked closely with the caterer and the bartender at each party to make

53

sure that, for example, the band plays soft, unobstrusive music when dinner is served. Mariano has never worked at the St. Germaine hotel.

Matisse has been the chef in the St. Germaine hotel restaurant for twelve years and is widely known for the wide range of tasty dishes he offers, from lasagna to Veal Cordon Bleu. The restaurant features a piano bar, and Matisse has been known to step out of the kitchen and sing to customers for whom he has prepared a special dish. When he last served Beef Stroganoff to a visiting Russian couple, he sent the customers a complimentary bottle of vodka and accompanied the waiter's entrance by bellowing the "Song of the Volga Boatmen." The restaurant accepts a few large parties (up to twelve people). Such parties often phone ahead days in advance to request that Matisse cook them a special dinner.

SECTION I: READING COMPREHENSION

Time: 35 Minutes
27 Questions

DIRECTIONS

Each passage in this group is followed by questions based on its content. After reading a passage, choose the best answer to each question and blacken the corresponding space on the answer sheet. Answer all questions following a passage on the basis of what is *stated* or *implied* in that passage. You may refer back to the passage.

Questions 1 through 7 are based on the following passage

The term "articulation disorder" refers to the difficulty an individual has when he uses the speech sounds of the language spoken around him. No communicative dysfunction is more familiar to the speech pathologist than the problem of misarticulation. Articulation disorders represent over two-thirds of the speech clinician's caseload; a rather sizable percentage when one considers that voice, rhythm, and language disorders also fall under this professional's purview.

Some individuals display difficulties in speech sound production due to organic factors, such as dysarthria, a neurological disorder, etc. Another factor that affects speech sound production is inadequate velopharyngeal closure, which can arise from (among other things) insufficient anatomical structure(s). These are disorders of concern to speech clinicians. However, the majority of individuals with articulatory defects treated by speech pathologists do not reveal difficulties arising from such factors. Quite frequently such problems for which no evidence of organic etiology or pathology can be found are termed "functional" articulation disorders. Admittedly, this is a vague term. "Functional articulation disorder" should be interpreted as a classification that indicates no evidence of organic involvement, in terms of our present knowledge.

A substantial proportion of articulation disorders fall into the "functional" category, and the question of what causes them is still a perplexing one. In-depth investigations have been con-

55

ducted to resolve the question of what organic, developmental, or environmental factors are related to articulatory difficulties. Winitz has presented a review of studies investigating the relationship between articulation and a number of these factors. While it appears that some factors are more related to articulation than others, it is fair to say that researchers have not yet identified any single causal factor that consistently relates to articulatory disorders. The task of identification and subsequent treatment of these functional articulation disorders falls within the speech clinician's responsibility.

The high incidence of articulatory disorders in young children suggests that such "disorders" may merely represent a developmental phenomenon. In general, the older the age, the lower the incidence of misarticulations. Speech clinicians are well aware of this fact. Typically, a child is not seen for articulation therapy unless he has difficulties using sounds that most children of the same age produce readily. This criterion for enrollment in therapy qualifies a substantial number of children for treatment. Yet longitudinal studies indicate that many of these "slow" children will show no difficulty using sounds several years later, even without treatment.

The usual defense for enrolling such a child in articulation therapy includes three points: (1) since some children do not "outgrow" their articulation problem, articulation therapy for all slowly developing children might be justified in order to insure that no child reaches adolescence with an articulation disorder, (2) misarticulations may represent a social stigma, and even though the articulation difficulties might be overcome in time without therapy, the concern for the child's social and emotional well-being might warrant the early articulation therapy, and (3) in cases where the articulation error has cosmetic disadvantages (e.g., lisping) without affecting the intelligibility of what is said, the speaker might continue speaking in the same manner because he is reinforced by the listener's comprehension. The longer this error is produced, however, the more difficult it might be to change.

Nevertheless, in this age of accountability, the fact that a large percentage of the speech clinician's time is spent with children who may overcome their articulatory difficulties without therapy does not rest well with many administrators. This situation has created a need, greater than ever before, for the development of therapeutic procedures that enable a child to acquire the use of speech sounds at a faster rate than he or she might acquire through maturation alone.

1. The passage implies that one of the factors contributing to the importance of articulation disorders is
   (A) the speech clinician's practice of treating nonserious disorders
   (B) the lack of organic causes of such disorders
   (C) the tendency of many children to "outgrow" the disorder
   (D) the high incidence of such disorders
   (E) the stress placed on such disorders by hospital administrators

2. According to the passage, any articulation disorder which is not purely "functional" may be
   (A) velopharyngeal   (D) etiological
   (B) organic   (E) pathological
   (C) dysarthriac

3. The author's attitude toward the efficacy of treatment for articulation disorders is
   (A) angry   (D) bemused
   (B) defensive   (E) neutral
   (C) skeptical

4. The author would probably agree with which of the following statements?
   (A) Adults do not suffer from articulation disorders.
   (B) Articulation therapy is useless.
   (C) Most afflicted with articulation disorders experience little discomfort.
   (D) Articulation disorders should not be investigated.
   (E) There may be no single causal factor that consistently relates to articulation disorders.

5. Which of the following titles is most appropriate for this passage?
  (A) Articulation Disorders
  (B) What Causes an Articulation Disorder?
  (C) Why Is an Articulation Disorder Treated?
  (D) Organic Disorders vs. Functional Disorders
  (E) Controversies Surrounding Treatment of Articulation Disorders

6. According to the passage, the need to develop more efficient therapeutic procedures is a result of
  (A) the increased need for clinical funding
  (B) the question of whether present procedures are always necessary
  (C) the increasing number of children whose disorders do not disappear
  (D) indications that the social stigma is stronger than ever
  (E) demands by clinicians

7. *Longitudinal* (paragraph 4) has which of the following meanings?
  (A) involving children who require a long time to express themselves
  (B) involving many children
  (C) lasting longer than necessary
  (D) conducted over an extensive period of time
  (E) confined to a specific geographic area

Questions 8 through 14 are based on the following passage

The term *euthanasia* is derived from the Greek word meaning "a good, or peaceful, death." Like abortion, euthanasia has received ever-increasing support, particularly during the last two decades, and its proponents demand profound changes in our individual, social, and moral attitudes toward death.

As a framework for the discussion of euthanasia in social education, it should be emphasized that two contemporary developments have resulted in forcing the subject of euthanasia to the forefront of social morality and ethics in modern societies. First, advanced technology has reached the level whereby the medical profession possesses a much wider range of choices between life and death. Second is the ever-increasing demands of the individual to maintain and exercise his rights over matters affecting his mental health, physical health, and his right to live or die.

With regard to the former, in technologically advanced societies, mere biological existence can be prolonged indefinitely by artificial life-supporting mechanisms. Sophisticated apparatus, new drugs, and the artificial transplantation of vital organs can give a new lease on life to persons who, in many instances, would rather die. From the standpoint of human rights, the depressing evidence concerning needless human suffering continues to prompt the idea that people, like animals, have the legal and moral right to a merciful death, or euthanasia.

Like abortion, the concept of legalizing the right to a merciful death has raised many significant moral, social, legal, and medical questions. The proposals to legalize voluntary euthanasia, under stringent conditions, have resulted in considerable criticism from organized Christianity. This is not surprising, since the sacredness of human life and personality is a fundamental tenet of the Christian faith. A basic concept for student awareness is that much of the criticism of euthanasia from organized religion, as well as other segments of society, involves both the relativity of the term and the negative precedent that legalized euthanasia could set for humanity.

Euthanasia, or mercy killing, is an idea that conjures up nearly as much fear as death itself among many. Indeed, it is one thing to translate the Greek word into "the good death"; it is another to be specific about such a benign term. Such questions arise as: Is it something you do to yourself: suicide? Is it something others do to you: murder? Could it be used as an excuse for genocide: the mass killing of the innocent, young or old, who happen to be a "political," "economic," or "racial" burden on a particular society? The racial theories and mass extermination practices of the Nazi period in Germany continue to haunt the Western world, and reinforce the fear of any legislation that could result in a repetition of this tragic era in contemporary history.

In its literal connotation, euthanasia, in the voluntary sense, reflects none of these social tragedies. Its legal and moral interpretation means that any individual who is incurably sick or miserably senile, whose condition is hopeless, and who desires to die, should be enabled to do so; and that he should be enabled to do so without his incurring, or his family incurring, or those who provide or administer the means of death incurring, any legal penalty or moral stigma whatsoever.

It is important for students to realize that the concept of euthanasia, like most contemporary controversial social themes, has been evolving for a long period. Nevertheless, in the United States, as in all societies, the power structures of both state and church have constantly rejected legislation deemed likely to result in the individual right of choice involving matters of life and death. The only way that governing establishments, until recent years, have been able to maintain their sovereignty in such matters has been to keep their inhabitants within the framework of legal and religious patterns that may have served society well at one time, but have now, largely as a result of technological advances, ceased to be useful to humanity. Throughout any discussion of euthanasia, it should continually be stressed that even though we are in many respects a violent society, reacting violently to various forms of official doctrine or human prejudice, we are also a nation in which capital punishment for major crimes is becoming increasingly rare.

8. The author implies that this essay's audience comprises which of the following groups?
   (A) students
   (B) physicians
   (C) proponents of euthanasia
   (D) critics of euthanasia
   (E) the terminally ill

9. According to the passage, the translation of *euthanasia* into "the good death" is inadequate because
   (A) death is never good
   (B) of the Greek tendency to oversimplify
   (C) that translation does not indicate many possible connotations of the term
   (D) it is implicitly associated with abortion
   (E) as societies become more advanced, euthanasia significantly changes its meaning

10. According to the passage, one of the factors that has established euthanasia as an important social issue is
    (A) a change in American lifestyles
    (B) its recognized relationship to capital punishment
    (C) a militant Christian movement against it
    (D) the threat of mass extermination
    (E) the number of individuals who insist upon making their own health decisions

11. The author provides information to answer which of the following questions?

     I. Should euthanasia be legalized?
    II. Can suicide be considered a type of euthanasia?
    III. Should those who practice euthanasia be punished?

        (A) I only
        (B) none of the above
        (C) I and II only
        (D) III only
        (E) I, II, and III

12. The primary purpose of this passage is to
    (A) argue for the social acceptance of euthanasia
    (B) argue against the social acceptance of euthanasia
    (C) summarize attitudes, questions, and definitions related to euthanasia
    (D) summarize the moral arguments for and against euthanasia
    (E) stress the rights of the individual

13. The author implies in the final paragraph that the decreased incidence of capital punishment
    (A) reflects the right of individuals to decide their own fate
    (B) has weakened national sovereignty
    (C) is not favored by the power structure
    (D) has not affected crimes of violence
    (E) reflects changing modern attitudes toward life and death

14. It can be inferred from the passage that euthanasia is a less important social issue in which of the following contexts?
    (A) a society which is not technologically advanced
    (B) a society which respects the rights of the individual
    (C) a society whose hospitals contain artificial life-supporting mechanisms
    (D) a Christian society
    (E) a society in which euthanasia carries a legal penalty

Questions 15 through 19 are based on the following passage

Laboratory evidence indicates that life originated through chemical reactions in the primordial mixture (water, hydrogen, ammonia, and hydrogen cyanide) which blanketed the earth at its formation. These reactions were brought about by the heat, pressure, and radiation conditions then prevailing. One suggestion is that nucleosides and amino acids were formed from the primordial mixture, and that nucleosides produced nucleotides which produced the nucleic acids (DNA, the common denominator of all living things, and RNA). The amino acids became polymerized (chemically joined) into proteins, including enzymes, and lipids were formed from fatty acids and glycerol-like molecules. The final step appears to have been the gradual accumulation of DNA, RNA, proteins, lipids, and enzymes into a vital mass which began to grow, divide, and multiply.

The evolution of the various forms of life from this biochemical mass must not be considered a linear progression. Rather, the fossil record suggests an analogy between evolution and a bush whose branches go every which way. Like branches, some evolutionary lines simply end, and others branch again. Many biologists believe the pattern to have been as follows: bacteria emerged first and from them branched viruses, red algae, blue-green algae, and green flagellates. From the latter branched green algae, from which higher plants evolved, and colorless rhizoflagellates, from which diatoms, molds, sponges, and protozoa evolved. From ciliated protozoa (ciliophora) evolved multinucleate (syncytial) flatworms. These branched into five lines, one of which leads to the echinoderms and chordates. The remaining lines lead to most of the other phyla of the animal kingdom.

Ostracoderms were the first vertebrates to evolve from the invertebrate stock of the chordate line, and from the ostracoderms, lampreys and placoderms evolved. Cartilaginous fish (sharks, skates, and rays) and bony fish evolved from the placoderms; and the crossopterygians (lobe-fin), which subsequently branched into the coelacanth and diplovertebron (an early amphibian), evolved from bony fish. The diplovertebron was the forerunner of modern amphibia and reptiles. The first reptiles, the cotylosaurs, branched into the unsuccessful dinosaurs and marine reptiles and into the successful turtles, crocodiles, birds, lizards, snakes, and mammals.

The line leading to man proceeds from the tree shrews to the early primates which branched into the New World monkeys, Old World monkeys, prongids, and hominids. From the prongids (true apes) came the gorilla, orangutan, and chimpanzee. From the hominids came contemporary man's immediate ancestor, Cro-Magnon man (Homo sapiens). Fossils of earlier "true men" (hominids that used tools) include East African man (Zinjanthropus) and Java ape man (Pithecanthropus).

15. Which of the following best expresses the analogy between evolution and a bush?
    (A) species : evolution : : bush : branching
    (B) species : branching : : bush : evolution
    (C) evolution : species : : bush : branched viruses
    (D) evolution : species : : bush : branches
    (E) evolution : species : : branches : bush

16. Nucleosides are predecessors of
    (A) polymers   (D) proteins
    (B) amino acids   (E) lipids
    (C) nucleic acids

17. Both dinosaurs and turtles are types of
    (A) successful reptiles   (D) mammals
    (B) unsuccessful reptiles   (E) hominids
    (C) cotylosaurs

18. It is likely that "New World monkeys" refer to monkeys that live in
    (A) fear of industrialization
    (B) new homes
    (C) newly founded African states
    (D) the United States
    (E) South America

19. The primordial mixture did not include
    (A) ammonia
    (B) hydrogen
    (C) heat
    (D) hydrogen cyanide
    (E) water

Questions 20 through 22 are based on the following passage

(1) Two separate worlds, that of the West and that of the East,
(2) had been established by the fourth century. Because of this
(3) split, the Eastern Empire, beginning with the foundation of
(4) Constantinople on the site of Byzantium, was called the By-
(5) zantine Empire. Still, its Greek-speaking inhabitants called
(6) themselves Romaioi (Romans) until its fall. The Eastern Em-
(7) pire proved to be stronger than its Western counterpart;
(8) there, the papacy filled a vacuum left by the disintegrating
(9) secular government. In the East, however, the central gov-
(10) ernment remained powerful, and the emperor appointed the
(11) Patriarchs of Constantinople and sometimes even dictated
(12) the tenets of Christian dogma. A large bureaucracy inherited
(13) from the Roman Empire was supported by intolerable taxes.
(14) At periods when there was no ruler (as in the Roman Em-
(15) pire, there were no succession laws), the empire was admin-
(16) istered by the bureaucrats.
(17)   In trying to reform the government, Justinian succeeded
(18) in reducing the number of bureaucrats, but taxes still re-
(19) mained high. Justinian's enduring achievement was his law

(20) code. Roman law originated from many sources such as
(21) praetorian edicts, imperial decrees, and jurisprudence (opin-
(22) ions and judgments of great lawyers). Under Theodosius II
(23) in 438 much of this legal heritage was codified, and under
(24) Justinian irrelevant and illogical laws were eliminated. The
(25) Code of Justinian (538) together with other legal documents
(26) made up the Body of Civil Law (Corpus Juris Civilis); it was
(27) modified in the eighth century according to certain Christian
(28) precepts, with fewer crimes made punishable by death. This
(29) Body of Civil Law is today the foundation for the law codes
(30) of many European states.
(31)   After the Roman conquest of the eastern region, the form
(32) of the Greek language (*koine*) prevalent during the Hellenis-
(33) tic and Roman periods continued in use. The Greek writers
(34) of the past were still studied and copied; indeed, the classics
(35) remained a living tradition in the Byzantine world. In the
(36) West, on the other hand, most Greek literary works were
(37) either lost or known only in abbreviated Latin translations.
(38) In any event, literacy had so declined there that only monks
(39) in the various religious orders were able to study Greek and
(40) Roman works, and they did so in only one context—as they
(41) related to Christianity. In the East Justinian closed the uni-
(42) versity at Athens because he felt it was too pagan, but the
(43) prestigious state university at Constantinople, founded by
(44) Theodosius II in 425, remained completely secular; both the
(45) liberal arts and sciences were studied there. Theology was
(46) studied at the School of the Patriarch of Constantinople. In
(47) addition to the clergy, therefore, the bureaucracy and the
(48) upper classes were literate in the East. In the field of litera-
(49) ture, there was continuity with a past that went back as far
(50) as Homer. The tradition of Greek lyric poetry continued as
(51) did that of epic. The most famous Byzantine epic of the
(52) eleventh century was Digenes Akritas; it concerned Byzan-
(53) tine warfare against Moslems and barbarians. In the twelfth
(54) century pastoral romances continued the tradition of Longus
(55) (third century). History was also an important Byzantine
(56) genre; the most famous Byzantine historians were Procopius,
(57) Psellus, and Anna Comnena. The secular intellectual life of
(58) the Byzantine period is also considered responsible for some
(59) of the most important literary criticisms of the classics, such
(60) as those of Tzetzes (twelfth century).

20. If each paragraph in this passage were given a title, the most accurate titles would be
    (A) "Patriarchs vs. the Pope," "The Codification of Laws," "Literary Traditions and Practices"
    (B) "Origins of the Byzantine Empire," "The Codification of Laws," "The Prevalence of *Koine*"
    (C) "Origins of the Byzantine Empire," "The Codification of Laws," "Literary Traditions and Practices"
    (D) "Origins of the Byzantine Empire," "The Failure of Tax Reform," "The Prevalence of *Koine*"
    (E) "Origins of the Byzantine Empire," "The Failure of Tax Reform," "Literary Traditions and Practices"

21. The word *there* in line 8 refers to
    (A) two separate worlds   (D) the papal vacuum
    (B) the Western Empire   (E) the seat of the Patriarchs
    (C) the Eastern Empire

22. It may be concluded that the Eastern and Western Empires were once united, and formed
    (A) a conglomerate of Greek Orthodox and Roman Catholic worshipers
    (B) the Old World
    (C) Homer's audience
    (D) the Ancient Roman Empire
    (E) the Ancient Russian Empire

Questions 23 through 27 are based on the following passage

Malinowski and other anthropologists have noted that some peoples, notably the Trobriand Islanders and the Australian Aborigines, are unaware of the role of the father in procreation. Most anthropologists accept the fact that almost universally social paternity is considered to be more important than the biological. Some peoples believe that the mother is but the carrier of the developing embryo, its actual flesh and blood coming from the father. Others believe that the menstrual flow nourishes the embryo; still others that it is the semen. In parts of Oceania, where the birth-rate is low, a woman may be required to give proof that she is fertile before she is permitted to marry.

Once pregnancy occurs, a woman may be required to eat certain foods that are believed to strengthen the baby within her or may have to perform certain activities to influence the growth of the baby. In the West, a pregnant woman is usually thought to be in a "delicate" condition whereas in other parts of the world she may be considered to be especially strong.

Men and unmarried females are frequently kept away from the vicinity of a birth. Often a woman returns to her mother's village for assistance during accouchement. Not all babies born are allowed to live. Infanticide is in many societies a factor in group survival, a technique of population control. Some peoples believe that twins are unnatural, thus they may be killed at birth. In some patrilineal groups, a baby without recognized paternity is not permitted to live. If a baby is born with the caul, he may be killed or perhaps be given a special status.

The couvade is a custom found among the Basques and in some parts of South America in which the father of a newborn child takes to bed and symbolically goes through the motions of parturition. In South America, the father's friends will pay him a visit, bringing him gifts and inquiring solicitously about his health. They are waited upon by the new mother.

Russians swaddle their babies because they believe that the babies are so strong and violent they might do harm to themselves unless secured in this way. Some American Indians think their babies will not grow up with straight, sturdy legs unless they are strapped to a board. In some societies babies are not allowed to cry. They are picked up immediately and satisfied or distracted. Other peoples consider that crying is a healthy exercise for the baby and allow him to cry for protracted periods.

A child learns about the ways of the society in which he was born from his playgroup. He will later transfer the experience gained in the primary group to the society at large. Very often patterns of authority are consistent throughout a culture, from parental to political to spiritual. A child is often disciplined by depriving him of that which he (or his society) prizes. Thus, one may learn what is held of value in a society. Rules of punishment teach much about the dominance-submission (superordination-subordination) attitudes of a society. In some societies every adult has authority over every child. In others the parent-child relationship is exclusive and not to be interfered with in any way.

In parts of the world where the life-spans are short, forty may be regarded as an advanced age. People who live longer are believed to possess special powers. These elders are sometimes treated with a deference based on fear rather than love.

In some societies, when death approaches, the dying person is moved out of the living quarters as a precaution against spiritual pollution. A corpse may be washed and dressed, perhaps painted and decorated, before being disposed of. In some cultures, corpses are placed where animals and the natural elements can get rid of the soft parts. In India bodies are usually cremated. The body may be buried in a seated or fetal position, facing camp or eastward, etc. Burial may be directly in the ground or in a coffin, tree trunk, large basket or pottery urn. Some peoples practice an initial interment of a year or so followed by a disinterment, the bones being collected at this time and placed elsewhere.

23. According to the passage, many societies regard certain types of childbearing as
    (A) sacred
    (B) joyful
    (C) unfortunate
    (D) harmless
    (E) normal

24. Which of the following might be most usefully supplied between paragraph 6 and paragraph 7?
    (A) a subtitle to indicate the beginning of an entirely new section
    (B) a transitional sentence indicating the author's shift from considering birth and life to considering age and death
    (C) a remention of specific practices of the Trobriand Islanders and the Australian Aborigines
    (D) a summary statement which particularly defines the unfamiliar words which have come before
    (E) an opinion by the author on the relative consequences of the beliefs sketched

25. The passage suggests that some areas try to assure population expansion by encouraging
    (A) premarital sex   (D) patrilinearity
    (B) polygamy   (E) couvade
    (C) menstruation

26. In some societies, infanticide is analogous to which of the following practices in our society?
    (A) murder   (D) black magic
    (B) vasectomy   (E) parturition
    (C) social Darwinism

27. At least one form of burial mentioned in the passage suggests a symbolic connection between
    (A) mother and father
    (B) birth and death
    (C) infanticide and genocide
    (D) embalming and cremation
    (E) civilization and primitivism

STOP. IF YOU FINISH BEFORE TIME IS CALLED, CHECK YOUR WORK ON THIS SECTION ONLY. DO NOT WORK ON ANY OTHER SECTION IN THE TEST.

SECTION II: ANALYTICAL REASONING

Time: 35 Minutes
26 Questions

DIRECTIONS

You will be presented several sets of conditions. A group of questions follows each set of conditions. Choose the best answer to each question, drawing a rough diagram of the conditions when necessary.

Questions 1 through 7 are based on the following statements

Ten figures (six numbers: 1, 2, 3, 4, 5, 6 and four letters: A, B, C, D) are listed in a line on a piece of paper.
The numbers are not necessarily in order, but the letters are in alphabetical order from left to right.
No two letters are next to each other.
The first two figures are 4 then 6, respectively.
D is between 1 and 3 and next to each of them.
2 is between B and C.

1. Which of the following must be false?

    I. C is between 1 and 2, and next to each.
   II. B is between 1 and A, and next to each.

  (A) I
  (B) II
  (C) either I or II but not both
  (D) both I and II
  (E) neither I nor II

2. Which of the following must be true?

    I. A is next to 6, but not next to 3.
   II. 5 is next to A, but not next to C.

  (A) I   (D) both I and II
  (B) II   (E) neither I nor II
  (C) either I or II but not both

71

3. If 3 is the last figure, then
   (A) B is next to 1
   (B) C is between 2 and 3, and next to each
   (C) A is between 4 and 6, and next to each
   (D) C is next to 1
   (E) D is next to 4

4. If the numbers next to B are added together, their total would be
   (A) 10   (B) 4   (C) 2   (D) 6   (E) 7

5. If someone wanted to add two more letters to the list, he or she
   (A) would have to put one letter between 4 and 6
   (B) would have to put one letter at the beginning
   (C) could not do so without breaking the rules
   (D) could do so only by rearranging the first four figures
   (E) would have to put both letters at the end

6. The letter that is most nearly in the center of the list is
   (A) A   (D) D
   (B) B   (E) cannot be determined
   (C) C

7. If you total the first two numbers in the list, they would be

   I. greater than the total of the last three numbers
   II. less than the total of the last three numbers
   III. twice the size of the third number

   (A) I   (D) I and II
   (B) II   (E) I and III
   (C) III

Questions 8 through 11 are based on the following statements

A family of nine consists of six children, two parents, and one grandparent.
Five of the six children have freckles.

Three children in the family are girls.
Four children in the family have blue eyes.
The parents both have blue eyes.

8. Which of the following must be true?

    I. All of the girls have freckles.
    II. At least one girl has blue eyes.

    (A) I
    (B) II
    (C) either I or II but not both
    (D) both I and II
    (E) neither I nor II

9. Which of the following must be false?

    I. All the blue-eyed girls have freckles.
    II. No children with freckles have blue eyes.

    (A) I
    (B) II
    (C) either I or II but not both
    (D) both I and II
    (E) neither I nor II

10. Which of the following can be deduced from the statements?
    (A) None of the girls have freckles.
    (B) Three of the blue-eyed children have freckles.
    (C) One girl has no freckles.
    (D) All of the girls have blue eyes.
    (E) none of the above

11. Which of the following must be false?
    (A) One of the children does not have freckles.
    (B) Three of the children are boys.
    (C) All of the boys have blue eyes.
    (D) Three children have brown eyes.
    (E) none of the above

Questions 12 through 19 are based on the following statements

Five students (Rich, Ron, Holly, Maria, and Sheila) receive different grades on an algebra test (A, B, C, D, and F, but not necessarily respectively).
Maria gets a lower grade than Holly.
Holly gets a lower grade than Rich.
Ron and Sheila do not get F's.
Rich gets the top grade.
Ron's grade is the average of Maria's and Rich's grades.

12. Which of the following must be true?

    I. Ron does not get an A.
    II. Sheila does not get a B.

    (A) I only
    (B) II only
    (C) either I or II but not both
    (D) both I and II
    (E) neither I nor II

13. Which of the following must be false?

    I. Rich cannot get a C.
    II. Maria gets an F.

    (A) I only
    (B) II only
    (C) either I or II but not both
    (D) both I and II
    (E) neither I nor II

14. Which statement is not deducible from the given information?
    (A) Rich gets an A.
    (B) Ron gets a C.
    (C) Sheila gets a lower grade than Holly.
    (D) Maria gets a lower grade than Holly.
    (E) Holly does not get an A.

15. If Holly gets a B, then

    I. Maria gets a C
   II. Sheila gets a D
  III. Ron gets an F

    (A) I
    (B) II
    (C) III
    (D) I and II
    (E) II and III

16. Which of the following must be true?

    I. Sheila cannot get a C.
   II. Maria cannot get a B.

  (A) I only
  (B) II only
  (C) both I and II
  (D) either I or II but not both
  (E) neither I nor II

17. Which of the following is determined by Sheila getting a B?
  (A) Rich getting an A
  (B) Ron getting a C
  (C) Holly getting a D
  (D) Maria getting an F
  (E) none of these

18. If Holly and Sheila were able to switch grades then
  (A) Holly would now get the B
  (B) Holly would now get the D
  (C) Sheila would now get the D
  (D) Sheila would now get the B
  (E) cannot be determined from given information

19. If Tom also took the test and received a grade with a "plus" or a "minus" (for instance B+ or A−) and Tom's grade was between Ron's grade and Holly's grade, then Tom could have gotten

   I. an A−
  II. a B−
 III. a C−

(A) I only   (D) I and II
(B) II only   (E) II and III
(C) III only

Questions 20 through 26 are based on the following statements

Sam is getting dressed to go to a party, but is having trouble deciding on what clothes to wear.

He will not wear any color combination that does not go well together.

He has two pairs of slacks, brown and blue; three dress shirts, white, aqua, and gray; four pairs of socks, red, black, brown, and blue; and two pairs of shoes, black and brown.

Blue slacks cannot be worn with red or brown socks.

Gray does not go well with brown.

Black does not go well with brown.

Assuming that Sam can wear only one pair of shoes, slacks, socks, and one shirt at a time, answer the following questions.

20. If Sam wears black shoes he will not wear
(A) blue socks   (D) blue slacks
(B) a white shirt   (E) red socks
(C) brown slacks

21. If Sam wears brown slacks and a white shirt, then

   I. he will not wear blue socks
  II. he will not wear black socks
 III. he could wear blue socks

(A) I   (D) I and II
(B) II   (E) II and III
(C) III

22. Sam will never wear
   (A) blue and red together
   (B) blue and brown together
   (C) white and black together
   (D) gray and blue together
   (E) white and red together

23. If color combinations did not matter, how many possible clothing combinations could Sam have?
   (A) 6   (B) 8   (C) 11   (D) 18   (E) 48

24. Sam buys a brown tie. Now he could wear

   I. a white shirt   III. blue socks
   II. brown slacks   IV. black shoes

   (A) I, III, and IV   (D) I, II, and III
   (B) I, II, and IV   (E) all of these
   (C) II, III, and IV

25. If Sam wears blue slacks, a white shirt, and brown shoes, then

         I. he cannot wear red socks
        II. he must wear blue socks
       III. he cannot wear black socks

   (A) I   (D) I and III
   (B) II   (E) I, II, and III
   (C) III

26. If Sam doesn't wear black socks or a gray shirt, then he could wear
   (A) red socks and blue slacks
   (B) brown socks and black shoes
   (C) brown shoes and brown slacks
   (D) brown slacks and black shoes
   (E) brown socks and blue slacks

STOP. IF YOU FINISH BEFORE TIME IS CALLED, CHECK YOUR WORK ON THIS SECTION ONLY. DO NOT WORK ON ANY OTHER SECTION IN THE TEST.

SECTION III: DISPUTE CHARACTERIZATION

Time: 35 Minutes
40 Questions

DIRECTIONS

You are presented with a narrative of facts, a dispute, and two rules. Sometimes the rules are conflicting, sometimes not; but in any case each rule should be considered independent of the other. Questions follow each set of rules. You are to classify each question according to the following choices:

(A) A relevant question whose answer requires a choice between the rules.

(B) A relevant question whose answer does not require a choice between the rules but requires additional facts or rules.

(C) A relevant question that is readily answerable from the facts or rules or both.

(D) An irrelevant question or one whose answer bears only remotely on the outcome of the dispute.

Set 1

Facts: Thad Nugget's backyard consisted of a very small patch of level ground, interrupted by a 60-degree incline which extended down to the highway 200 feet below. At the bottom of the incline was a chain link fence running along the side of the road. Nugget decided to convert the incline into a water slide and constructed a long slide leading to a deep swimming pool. After inspecting the water slide and pool, the city certified it but restricted it to private use. One summer morning, Del Acorn was driving down the highway when one of his tires blew out and he lost control of his car. The car crashed through Nugget's fence, with both auto and driver suffering only minor damage at that point. But Acorn was unable to stop the vehicle, and it plummeted into the swimming pool. Acorn escaped from the car and pulled himself out of the water, but the automobile submerged completely and the damage was irreparable.

Dispute: Acorn sued Nugget for the damages to his car. Nugget contested.

Rule I: A homeowner cannot be liable for damages caused by his or her property if that property has been certified by the city and is used as authorized.

Rule II: A homeowner is liable for any damages occurring on his or her property.

Questions:

1. How long was Nugget's fence?
2. If Nugget was using the pool as authorized, will Acorn win the suit?
3. If Nugget was renting the slide and the pool for public use, who will win the suit?
4. Where did the damages occur?
5. If Nugget was leasing the property, would he be liable for the damages occurring on it?
6. Why were the slide and pool restricted to private use only?

Set 2

Facts: In 1979 the Earthfood vitamin manufacturers began distributing vitamins to the Health City chain of natural food stores, which sold the vitamins under the label Stamina-Plus. In 1980, Earthfood expanded its business by opening its own chain of natural food stores and selling its vitamins for half the price charged by Health City, which continued to sell the Stamina-Plus brand manufactured by Earthfood. The vitamins sold in the Earthfood stores were identical to those sold by Health City, but the brand name adopted by Earthfood was Strength-Plus. In 1982, Earthfood stores began advertising the low cost and high quality of its vitamins in national magazines, stating that those people taking Strength-Plus vitamins reported better results than those taking Stamina-Plus vitamins.

Dispute: Health City sued Earthfood for false advertising. Earthfood contested.

Rule I: One is guilty of false advertising if one cannot substantiate written claims with factual data.

Rule II: One is guilty of false advertising only if the false representation was intentional.

Questions:

7. If the representation was false, will the cost of the advertisements have a bearing on the dispute?
8. Could Earthfood substantiate its written claims with factual data?
9. If their representation was false but not intentional, is Earthfood guilty of false representation?
10. Was Health City successful in their advertising?
11. If the Earthfood claim is false and intentional, will Earthfood win?
12. If the Earthfood claim was true and could be substantiated with factual data, who will win?

Set 3

Facts: Sal had contracted Brian to paint his house. Brian spilled some turpentine around his work area, a common occurrence in painting, just as Sal's watchdog, Rocky, came trotting by. Rocky stepped in the turpentine unbeknownst to Sal and began licking his paws in order to clean off the foreign material. Three days later, Sal noticed that Rocky's tongue was severely inflamed and swollen and rushed him to a veterinarian. The vet treated the pet and billed Sal for the amount. Soon after the incident, Brian came to collect his painting fee from Sal. When Sal told him what had happened to Rocky, Brian recalled that Rocky had stepped in the turpentine but added that he doubted that a small amount of turpentine could cause such a serious inflammation. Sal accused Brian of carelessly endangering his dog's life.

Dispute: Sal sued Brian for damages. Brian contested.

Rule I: Unless previously stipulated, a contractee is not liable for damages resulting from ordinary circumstances of his or her employment.

Rule II: A contractee is liable for any damages over $300 which he or she causes.

Questions:

13. Was there a previous stipulation in the contract regarding liabilities?
14. Did the damages exceed $300?
15. If the damages were for $200 and there were no contract stipulations regarding liability, will Brian win the suit?
16. If the damages were for $350 and there were no contract stipulations regarding liability, will Brian win the suit?
17. Was the painting fee exorbitant?
18. If spilling turpentine was not ordinary circumstances of his employment and the damages were for $350, will Sal win?

Set 4

Facts: Doris answered her door one Saturday to find her new neighbor, Frank Depot, holding a small portable television set. Frank said that he had purchased the set at a swap meet that morning but became worried because the seller had informed him that the television was stolen property. Frank asked Doris her legal opinion of the matter, and she advised him to turn the set in to the police, who would try to return it to its rightful owner. Frank asked if Doris would accompany him to the police station. She refused, but promised to call the desk sergeant and use her influence to see that Frank was treated fairly. Doris phoned the police and told them she suspected Frank of larceny. When Frank arrived at the police station with the television, he was subjected to intense questioning by the detectives, who eventually arrested him on suspicion of larceny.

Dispute: Frank was arraigned for the crime of larceny. He contested.

Rule I: One who knowingly buys stolen property is guilty of the crime of larceny.

Rule II: One who is in possession of stolen property but returns it to the owner or police is not guilty of a crime.

Questions:

19. If Frank did not return the property, was he guilty of the crime of larceny?
20. If Frank was informed that the television was stolen after he made the purchase, will he be found guilty?
21. What was the value of the television?
22. Did Frank know that the property was stolen before the purchase was made?
23. If Frank knew that the TV was stolen before he made the purchase, will he be found guilty?

Set 5

Facts: D. L. Duckworth, owner of All World Pools, a large swimming pool building company, had been having a slow summer when Jay Pennypincher approached him about a reduced rate on installing a pool. Since business had been slow, Duckworth agreed to build and install the pool within 30 days for a price that was far below his cost, just to maintain a positive cash flow. Duckworth, realizing business was bad all over, decided to subcontract parts of the job to local contractors, describing the job to them and having them bid on the job sight unseen. Having given the job to the lowest bidder, Flacme Pool Installers, Duckworth signed an agreement for them to complete the job in the allotted time. When the Flacme workers arrived at Pennypincher's house, they realized that they had tremendously underbid the job. The job was not what had been described and would take them twice as long to finish. Flacme Pool Installers refused to start work. Pennypincher, hearing of this refusal, went to another company and had the pool installed.

Dispute: Duckworth sued Pennypincher for breaking the contract. Pennypincher contested.

Rule I: A written contract between two parties is enforceable and may not be terminated unless there is adequate cause to believe that one will not fulfill part of the agreement.

Rule II: Any contract may be voided verbally or in writing by either party within three days of the signing of the agreement, as long as the work has not been completed or the contract fulfilled before that time.

Questions:

24. If Pennypincher phoned Duckworth five days later and broke the contract, will Duckworth win the suit?
25. Did Pennypincher have adequate cause to believe that Duckworth would not fulfill his part of the agreement?
26. If Flacme had carefully estimated the project before making their bid, was their bid fair?
27. Did Pennypincher have the pool installed by All World Pools?
28. If the contract was in writing and if Pennypincher had adequate cause to believe that the agreement would not be fulfilled and notified Duckworth within three days, will Pennypincher win the suit?
29. If Pennypincher phoned Duckworth and broke the written contract the day after it was signed but did not have adequate cause to do so, who will win the suit?

Set 6

Facts: Bill Brown and Sue Green were planning to be married on August 5th. The night before, at the wedding rehearsal, Bill and Sue had an argument. Bill followed Sue home into the next county, broke into her house, and continued the argument. Sue then told Bill that she no longer would consider marrying him. This enraged Bill even more, and he smashed Sue's 19″ color television set. On the way to his car, Bill also poured a box of sugar, which he took from Sue's cupboard, directly into the gas tank of Sue's new sports car. The sports car's engine was ruined.

Dispute: Sue sued Bill for damages for the TV and the car. Bill contested, pleading temporary insanity.

Rule I: Temporary insanity vindicates the assailant but can be claimed only when the assailant is so enraged that he or she has no comprehension of the extent or severity of his or her actions.

Rule II: An assailant is responsible and liable for his or her actions.

Questions:

30. Was Bill temporarily insane when he committed the actions?
31. If Bill was temporarily insane and had no comprehension of the extent or severity of his actions, will Sue win the suit?
32. Did Bill know what effect sugar would have on the car?
33. If Bill did comprehend the extent or severity of his actions, will he win the suit?
34. How severe were the damages to the TV?

Set 7

Facts: After a local citizens group complained that the intersection of Lichtenstein Avenue and Senator Street was unusually dangerous, the city put up a four-way stop sign. All of the residents were very happy about this, except Nan Dodger, who enjoyed coasting her car down the steep Senator Street hill through the intersection, halting crosstraffic and always risking a collision. One afternoon, Nan decided to defy the stop sign and coast through the intersection anyway. When she was about 200 feet short of the intersection, Nan saw a large moving van, owned and driven by Mike Triceps of Tri-Quality Movers, proceeding through the intersection directly across her path. Immediately applying the brakes, Nan passed the stop sign but was able to stop just a few feet short of colliding with Mike. When Mike saw Nan's car approaching, he accelerated to try to clear the intersection. This caused several of the boxes which he had loosely packed to tumble over inside the truck. Six glass lamps were broken.

Dispute: Tri-Quality Movers sued Nan for the cost of the lamps. Nan contested.

Rule I: One is liable for any damages if he or she causes the damages by breaking the law.

Rule II: Damages caused by negligence must be paid for by the negligent party.

Questions:

35. Was Mike negligent in packing?
36. If Mike was not negligent, will he win the suit?
37. How effective was the four-way stop?
38. If Mike was negligent but Nan wasn't, will Tri-Quality be reimbursed by Nan?
39. Were there any damages?
40. Did Mike stop at the stop sign?

STOP. IF YOU FINISH BEFORE TIME IS CALLED, CHECK YOUR WORK ON THIS SECTION ONLY. DO NOT WORK ON ANY OTHER SECTION IN THE TEST.

SECTION IV: LOGICAL REASONING

Time: 35 Minutes
26 Questions

DIRECTIONS

You will be presented with brief passages or statements and will be required to evaluate their reasoning. In each case, select the best answer choice, even though more than one choice may present a possible answer. Choices which are unreasonable or incompatible with common-sense standards should be eliminated.

1. Which of the following most logically completes the passage at the blank below?

The English language, lacking the rigidity of most European tongues, has been bent and shaped in at least as many ways as there are countries or regions where it is spoken. Though purists often argue that "standard" English is spoken only in certain high-minded enclaves of the American northeast, the fact is that it is the most widely used language in the world and is not likely to yield that distinction for a very long time, if ever. Nevertheless, _____.

   (A) it remains one of the most widely spoken languages throughout the world
   (B) it can be understood in just about every corner of the globe
   (C) even making allowances for regional peculiarities, English as it is spoken has been much abused in recent times
   (D) though we may be proud of these facts, English remains one of the most difficult languages to master
   (E) English, as it is spoken, lacks the rigidity of the classical and more historic European languages

2. Life imitates art.

Which of the following, if true, most strongly supports the above statement?

   (A) When Warren Beatty filmed *Reds,* he tried to suggest not only the chaos of the Russian Revolution but also its relationship to the present.

   (B) The number of professional ballet companies has increased over the last five years, but the number of dance majors has decreased.

   (C) On Tuesday, the business section of the newspaper had predicted the drop in interest rates that occurred on Friday.

   (D) Truman Capote wrote *In Cold Blood* as a result of a series of brutal slayings by two crazed killers.

   (E) Soon after the advent of color television, white shirts became less popular as dressy attire for men, and pastel-colored shirts began to sell well.

   When President Lyndon Johnson signed the Voting Rights Act in 1965, he used fifty pens, handing them out as souvenirs to a joyous gathering in the President's Room of the Capitol, where Abraham Lincoln had signed the Emancipation Proclamation on January 1, 1863. When President Reagan signed an extension of the Voting Rights Act in 1982, he spoke affectionately of "the right to vote," signed with a single pen, then concluded the four-minute ceremony by rising from his desk, announcing, "It's done."

3. If the passage above is true, which of the following is most probably true?

   (A) The Voting Rights Act did not require an extension.

   (B) The Voting Rights Act is not significantly related to the Emancipation Proclamation.

   (C) President Reagan saw himself as more like Lincoln than did Johnson.

   (D) President Reagan did not regard the extension of the act as an occasion for fanfare.

   (E) President Reagan objected strenuously to an extension of the Voting Rights Act.

4. *Congressman:* Serving a few months as a Capitol page can be an exciting and enriching experience for high school students from around the country.

   Student: If the circumstances are right.

The student's response suggests which of the following?

(A) belligerence   (D) disbelief

(B) acquiescence   (E) ignorance

(C) skepticism

Questions 5 and 6 refer to the passage below

On average, federal workers receive salaries 35.5 percent higher than private-sector salaries. For instance, federal workers in California average $19,206 a year, 25 percent higher than the average pay in the private sector, which is $15,365.

5. This information would best support which of the following opinions?

   (A) Private-sector salaries in California are above average.

   (B) The private sector is being paid fairly.

   (C) Federal jobs are more secure than private-sector jobs.

   (D) Public-sector work is more difficult than private-sector work.

   (E) Federal pay is out of line.

6. Which of the following statements is consistent with the information in the passage?

   (A) Salaries of California federal workers more nearly approximate the salaries in the private sector than do the salaries of federal workers nationwide.

   (B) There are more generous vacation leave privileges for private workers than for federal workers.

   (C) Social programs have been curtailed in the face of large state deficits.

   (D) State workers in California receive salaries comparable to those of private workers.

   (E) Recently, federal workers have begun demanding higher compensation benefits.

Money talks as never before in state and local elections, and the main cause is TV advertising. Thirty seconds can go as high as $2000. Political fundraising is one of the few growth industries left in America. The way to stop the waste might be for television to be paid by state and local government, at a standard rate, to provide air time to all candidates to debate the issues. This might be boring at first. But eventually candidates might actually brush up their debating skills and electrify the TV audience with content, not style.

7. Which of the following presuppositions is (are) necessary to the argument above?

   I. Candidates spend too much money on television advertising.
  II. Television can be used to educate and inform the public.
 III. The freedom of speech doesn't abridge the freedom to spend.

(A) I only
(B) II only
(C) III only
(D) I and II
(E) I, II, and III

Questions 8 and 9 refer to the following passage

According to a recent study by the National Academy of Public Administration, postal patrons are regularly affronted by out-of-order stamp vending machines, branch post office lobbies locked at night, and twenty-cent letters that take as long to get there as eight-cent letters did a decade ago.

8. Which of the following, if true, would weaken the implication of one of the writer's observations?
(A) Most out-of-order vending machines are located in rundown neighborhoods.
(B) Late-night vandalism has plagued post offices nationwide.
(C) Postage rates rose 88 percent from 1971 to 1980, but the cost of first class mail is still cheaper in the U.S. than anywhere else.
(D) As a public corporation, the Postal Service has increased its capital assets by $3 billion.

(E) Ten years ago, most letters reached their destination within twenty-four hours.

9. Which of the following transitions probably begins a sentence critical of the argument above?
(A) However
(B) In addition
(C) Despite
(D) In reality
(E) Therefore

Of all the petty little pieces of bureaucratic arrogance, it's hard to imagine one smaller than that of the city schools in not admitting a British subject whose father is working—as a legal alien—for a nearby petrochemical company. Someone apparently decided that if the boy had been an illegal alien, a recent U.S. Supreme Court decision in a Texas case would have required the district to admit him, but since he is legal, there is no such requirement. That is nonsense.

10. Which of the following best expresses the point of the author's argument?
(A) The city schools outside Texas should not base decisions on a precedent set in Texas.
(B) The stability of a parent's job should have no bearing on the educational opportunity offered his or her child.
(C) Bureaucratic arrogance has resulted in unsound legal interpretation.
(D) Legal sense and nonsense are sometimes indistinguishable.
(E) Both legal and illegal aliens should receive equal treatment.

By appropriating bailout money for the depressed housing industry, Congress is opening the door to a flood of special relief programs for other recession-affected businesses.

11. The author's attitude toward Congress's action is probably
(A) neutral
(B) disapproving
(C) confused
(D) happy
(E) irate

A researcher has concluded that women are just as capable as men in math but that their skills are not developed because society expects them to develop other and more diverse abilities.

12. Which of the following is a basic assumption of the researcher?
    (A) Ability in math is more important than ability in more diverse subjects.
    (B) Ability in math is less important than ability in more diverse subjects.
    (C) Women and men should be equally capable in math.
    (D) Women might be more capable than men in math.
    (E) Women tend to conform to social expectations.

Questions 13 and 14 refer to the following passage

Beginning this fall, Latino and Asian students will not be allowed to transfer out of bilingual classes (that is, a program in which courses are given in a student's native language) until they pass strict competency tests in math, reading, and writing—as well as spoken English. The board and its supporters say this will protect children from being pushed out of bilingual programs before they are ready. They have hailed this as a victory for bilingual education.

13. Which of the following, if true, is the strongest criticism of the position of the board?
    (A) A foreign student may be quite competent in math without being competent in English.
    (B) Some native students already in English-speaking classes are unable to pass the competency tests.
    (C) Most foreign students require many months of practice and instruction before mastering English skills.
    (D) Many students prefer to transfer out of bilingual classes before they have achieved competency in English.
    (E) Holding back students will double the number of students in bilingual classes—twice as many Latino and Asian children isolated from the English-speaking mainstream.

14. The argument above would be most strengthened if the author were to explain
    (A) how efficient the bilingual program is
    (B) how well staffed the bilingual program is
    (C) whether the community supports the bilingual program
    (D) whether any board members do not support the bilingual program
    (E) how the students feel about the bilingual program

The $464 million "reserve" in the 1982–83 budget adopted by the legislature in June turns out to have been based mainly on wishful thinking. Because of tax cuts approved by voters on the June ballot, along with the continuing recession and other events affecting income and expenses, the actual reserve in prospect may be as low as $7 million.

15. The author is probably leading to which of the following conclusions?
    (A) These facts warrant an investigation into who squandered $457 million.
    (B) A reserve in the budget is not so necessary as we might wish it to be.
    (C) The legislature would be wise not to add any new spending to the budget adopted in June.
    (D) The recession will probably not last much longer, but while it does the legislature must adjust the budget accordingly.
    (E) Legislative budgets are typically careless and unheeding of variable factors which may affect their accuracy.

Questions 16 and 17 refer to the following passage

"The sum of behavior is to retain a man's dignity without intruding upon the liberty of others," stated Sir Francis Bacon. If this is the case, then not intruding upon another's liberty is impossible.

16. The conclusion strongly implied by the author's arguments is that
    (A) retaining one's dignity is impossible without intruding upon another's liberty
    (B) retaining dignity never involves robbing others of liberty
    (C) dignity and liberty are mutually exclusive
    (D) there is always the possibility of a "dignified intrusion"
    (E) B. F. Skinner's *Beyond Freedom and Dignity* takes its cue from Bacon

17. The author's argument would be weakened if it were pointed out that

    I. Bacon's argument has been misinterpreted out of context
    II. neither liberty nor dignity can be discussed in absolute terms
    III. retaining dignity always involves a reduction of liberty

    (A) I, II, and III   (D) II and III only
    (B) III only   (E) I and II only
    (C) I only

   Jonathan Swift said, "Laws are like cobwebs which may catch small flies but let wasps and hornets break through."

18. Jonathan Swift would most probably believe that
    (A) prosecutors should be tough on criminals
    (B) pesticides should be used to deter large insects
    (C) small crimes should not be prosecuted
    (D) the powerful can often avoid serious criminal sentences
    (E) laws do not stop people from committing crimes

19. Which of the following most logically completes the passage at the blank below?

   In a civilized society, members of the community will often defer to others, even against their own better judgment. This situation may occur in public, in gatherings with strangers, or in the household with one's family or friends. It is a sign of a more sophisticated culture that one's immediate interests are thought to be secondary to those of another. On first examination this may seem to be selflessness, but _____.

(A) actually it is not; it is just ignorance
(B) rather it may take many names
(C) actually it is
(D) to some extent it does serve the ends of the individual concerned
(E) sometimes it can harbor animosities and hostility

Questions 20 through 23 refer to the following passage

The older we get, the less sleep we should desire. This is because our advanced knowledge and capabilities are most enjoyable when used; therefore, "mindless" sleep becomes a waste of time.

20. Which of the following distinctions is *not* expressed or implied by the author?
(A) between sleep and wakefulness
(B) between youth and maturity
(C) between productivity and waste
(D) between a desire and a requirement
(E) between more sleep and less sleep

21. The author of this statement assumes that
(A) less sleep is not desirable
(B) sleep advances knowledge and capabilities
(C) mindlessness coincides with wakefulness
(D) knowledge and capabilities naturally improve with age
(E) sleep is only for the young

22. This author's statement might be strengthened if he or she pointed out that
(A) advanced knowledge is often manifested in creative dreams
(B) the mind is quite active during sleep
(C) few empirical studies have concluded that sleep is an intellectual stimulant
(D) advanced capabilities are not necessarily mind-associated
(E) dreams teach us how to use waking experiences more intelligently

23. The author's statement might be weakened by pointing out that
    (A) eight hours of sleep is a cultural, not a physical, require-
        ment
    (B) the most capable people rarely sleep
    (C) rest is a positive contribution to knowledge and capability
    (D) young children enjoy themselves less than knowledgeable
        adults
    (E) people rarely waste time during their waking hours

  Don't spend the night tossing and turning! Take Eezy-Z's for
a sound, restful sleep . . . you'll wake up refreshed, energized,
with no drugged-up hangover. Remember . . . Eezy-Z's when
you need that sleep!

24. Which of the following is *not* a claim of Eezy-Z's?
    (A) a good night's sleep   (D) quickly falling asleep
    (B) added energy   (E) a restful slumber
    (C) no aftereffects

  On a swimming team—
    All freestyle swimmers are Olympic winners.
    No blue-eyed swimmer is an Olympic winner.
    All Olympic winners go on to lucrative professional careers.

25. If it is determined that all of the above are true, then which of the
    following must also be true about the swimming team?
    (A) All those who go on to professional careers are freestyle
        swimmers.
    (B) Only freestyle swimmers go on to professional careers.
    (C) Some blue-eyed swimmers go on to lucrative professional
        careers.
    (D) No blue-eyed swimmer is a freestyle swimmer.
    (E) Only blue-eyed swimmers don't go on to lucrative careers.

  Dear Sir or Madam:

  Up until last Sunday I was very pleased with the Stanford
Brand Auto Polisher that I purchased at your store several years

ago. Unfortunately, as I was using it on my $15,000 sports car, the waxing head flew off and smashed my windshield. In addition, when the head dislodged, the underworkings caused a large scratch on the front fender, which will cost an additional $300 to fix. I herewith enclose damage costs, as well as request replacement costs for the Stanford Brand Auto Polisher, which is under warrantee. (I will send you a copy of the twelve-month guarantee form that I filled out upon purchase).

I look forward to hearing from you.

Sincerely,

P.R. Knockridge

26. Which of the following is an essential condition which the writer of the letter fails to realize?
    (A) Knockridge's letter should have been dated.
    (B) Standord Brand products, and not the store, will provide the replacements or damage costs.
    (C) The twelve-month guarantee is no longer valid.
    (D) A copy of the warrantee should have been included.
    (E) Estimates of the damage should have been included.

STOP. IF YOU FINISH BEFORE TIME IS CALLED, CHECK YOUR WORK ON THIS SECTION ONLY. DO NOT WORK ON ANY OTHER SECTION IN THE TEST.

SECTION V: ANALYTICAL REASONING

Time: 35 Minutes
26 Questions

DIRECTIONS

You will be presented several sets of conditions. A group of questions follows each set of conditions. Choose the best answer to each question, drawing a rough diagram of the conditions when necessary.

Questions 1 through 6 refer to the following statements

Liz, Jenni, Jolie, and Rick have an English final on Friday and they all would like to study together at least once before the test.
Liz can study only on Monday, Tuesday, and Wednesday nights, and Thursday afternoon and night.
Jenni can study only on Monday, Wednesday, and Thursday nights, and Tuesday afternoon and night.
Jolie can study only on Wednesday and Thursday nights, Tuesday afternoon, and Monday afternoon and night.
Rick can study the afternoons and nights of Tuesday, Wednesday, and Thursday, and on Monday afternoon.

1. If the group is to study twice, then the days could be
   (A) Monday and Wednesday   (D) Monday and Friday
   (B) Tuesday and Thursday   (E) Tuesday and Wednesday
   (C) Wednesday and Thursday

2. If three of them tried to study together when all four couldn't,
   (A) this would be possible twice
   (B) it would have to be on Wednesday night
   (C) Rick could not attend the three-person groups
   (D) this could be accomplished on Monday and Tuesday only
   (E) this would not be possible

99

3. If Liz decided to study every night,
   (A) she would never be able to study with Rick
   (B) she would never be able to study with Jolie
   (C) she would have at least two study partners each night
   (D) she would have to study alone on Monday night
   (E) she would study with only Jenni on Thursday night

4. If the test were moved up to Thursday morning, which of the following must be true?

   I. The complete group would not be able to study together.
   II. Liz could never study in the afternoon.
   III. Jolie and Jenni could study together three times.

   (A) I only   (D) II and II only
   (B) I and II only   (E) I, II, and III
   (C) I and III only

5. Dan wants to join the study group. If the larger study group is to be able to study all together then Dan will have to be available on
   (A) Wednesday night   (D) Monday night
   (B) Thursday afternoon   (E) Wednesday afternoon
   (C) Tuesday night

6. Which student is available to study at a time when no other student is available?
   (A) Liz   (D) Rick
   (B) Jenni   (E) none of these
   (C) Jolie

Questions 7 through 14 refer to the following statements

Two women, Amy and Carla, and two men, Bernard and Doug, are doctors. One is a dentist, one a surgeon, one an optometrist, and one a general practitioner. They are seated around a square table with one person on each side.

1. Bernard is across from the dentist.
2. Doug is not across from the surgeon.

3. The optometrist is on Amy's left.
4. Carla is the general practitioner.
5. The surgeon and general practitioner are married to each other.
6. The general practitioner is not on Carla's left.
7. The general practitioner is across from the optometrist.

7. Which statement is repeated information?
   (A) 1   (B) 5   (C) 6   (D) 7   (E) none of these

8. Which of the following must be false?

   I. Bernard is the dentist.
   II. The surgeon and general practitioner are women.
   III. The dentist is across from the surgeon.

   (A) I   (D) I and II
   (B) II   (E) II and III
   (C) III

9. Which of the following must be true?

   I. Two women sit next to each other.
   II. Two men sit across from each other.

   (A) I only
   (B) II only
   (C) both I and II
   (D) either I and II but not both
   (E) neither I nor II

10. Which of the following must be true?

    I. Doug is the optometrist.
    II. The surgeon and general practitioner sit next to each other.

    (A) I only
    (B) II only
    (C) both I and II
    (D) either I or II but not both
    (E) neither I nor II

11. Which of the following is true?
    (A) Doug is the general practitioner.
    (B) Bernard is the surgeon.
    (C) Carla is the dentist.
    (D) Amy is the optometrist.
    (E) none of the above

12. Which of the following must be true?
    I. Doug is the optometrist.
    II. Amy is the dentist.
    III. Both men sit opposite a woman.

    (A) I only   (D) I and II
    (B) II only   (E) I, II, and III
    (C) III only

13. If Bernard and Amy switch seats, then
    (A) Carla sits across from Amy
    (B) Doug sits across from Bernard
    (C) Bernard sits across from Amy
    (D) Carla sits next to Doug
    (E) Amy sits next to Bernard

14. If both men leave the table,
    (A) the optometrist and dentist remain
    (B) the surgeon and optometrist remain
    (C) the surgeon and general practitioner remain
    (D) the general practitioner and dentist remain
    (E) not enough information to tell

Questions 15 through 19 refer to the following statements

The mythical countries of Bongo and Congo are exactly square shaped and lie next to each other in an east-west direction, though not necessarily in that order. Their common border spans the width of both countries. The capital city of one of the countries is "A." It lies due east from the other capital, "B."

"C" is the border city of Congo, on the Bongo boundary.

"D" is the harbor city of Bongo for ships coming from the west.

"E" is the easternmost city of Bongo.

"F" is 27 miles due west of Congo's capital city, in Congo.

The main highway, Bongo-Congo 1, goes from "B" eastward to the coastal city of "G."

15. Going east to west a traveler would encounter cities in which order?
    (A) G, A, E, C, F   (D) G, A, F, C, E
    (B) A, F, C, B, E   (E) C, B, E, F, A
    (C) D, B, E, C, F

16. When the sun rises, the first city to see it is
    (A) G   (B) F   (C) B   (D) E   (E) D

17. When the sun sets, the last city to see it is
    (A) G   (B) F   (C) B   (D) E   (E) D

18. Which of the following is (are) true?

    I. "B" is the capital city of Bongo.
    II. "A" is the capital city of Congo.
    III. "C" is the last Bongo city encountered on the way to Congo.

    (A) I   (D) I and II
    (B) II   (E) II and III
    (C) III

19. Which statement is true of city "E"?
    (A) It is the easternmost city of the easternmost country.
    (B) It is the westernmost city of the westernmost country.
    (C) It is the easternmost city of the westernmost country.
    (D) It is the westernmost city of the easternmost country.
    (E) It is due west of Bongo's capital city.

Questions 20 through 26 refer to the following statements

1. A small elevator starts at the first floor with three people and stops at the fifth floor with five people.
2. The elevator can accommodate only five people at any one time.
3. The elevator makes only three stops, including the destination.
4. On this trip, the elevator goes only up.
5. The elevator can hold only 1,000 pounds or it breaks.
6. Three people get on at the second floor.

20. Which of the following must be true?
    (A) At least one person gets off on the second floor.
    (B) At least two persons get off on the second floor.
    (C) No one gets off on the third floor.
    (D) Only one person gets off on the second floor.
    (E) At least one person gets on on the third floor.

21. Which of the following must be true?
    (A) Only one person on the elevator weighed over 250 pounds.
    (B) Six people could get on the elevator.
    (C) Each person getting on the elevator at the first stop weighed less than 150 pounds.
    (D) The average weight of the people at the fifth floor did not exceed 200 pounds.
    (E) none of the above

22. Which of the following must be false?
    I. The elevator stops at the third floor.
    II. No one gets off at the second floor.
    III. No one gets on at the fourth floor.

    (A) I only   (D) I and II
    (B) II only   (E) II and III
    (C) III only

23. If two people get off at the second floor and four get on at the third floor, what happened at the fourth floor?
    (A) Two people get off.
    (B) One person gets off and two get on.
    (C) Three people get off and two get on.
    (D) Five people get off and five people get on.
    (E) The elevator doesn't stop.

24. If the elevator doesn't stop at the second floor and no people get off at the third or fourth floors, then which could be true?

    I. One person gets on at each, floor 3 and floor 4.
    II. Three people get on at floors 3 and 4.

    (A) I only   (D) neither I nor II
    (B) II only   (E) cannot be determined
    (C) I and II

25. If at the fifth floor, two people get on, then
    (A) three people get off
    (B) everyone gets off
    (C) at least one person gets off
    (D) two people get off
    (E) at least two people get off

26. If another stop is added to the trip, and the above "rules" (except rule 3) are still obeyed, then which of the following could be true?

    I. The elevator stops again at the second floor.
    II. Three people get off at the sixth floor.
    III. Six 200-pound people get off at the seventh floor.

    (A) I only   (D) I and II
    (B) II only   (E) I, II, and III
    (C) III only

STOP. IF YOU FINISH BEFORE TIME IS CALLED, CHECK YOUR WORK ON THIS SECTION ONLY. DO NOT WORK ON ANY OTHER SECTION IN THE TEST.

SECTION VI: READING COMPREHENSION

Time: 35 Minutes
28 Questions

DIRECTIONS

Each passage in this group is followed by questions based on its content. After reading a passage, choose the best answer to each question and blacken the corresponding space on the answer sheet. Answer all questions following a passage on the basis of what is *stated* or *implied* in that passage. You may refer back to the passage.

Questions 1 through 7 refer to the following passage

In addition to determining whether or not a child's misarticulations require therapy, the speech clinician must also determine which of several misarticulated sounds should be treated first. One of the most common criteria for sound selection is developmental age. If a child is misarticulating several sounds, the clinician will frequently select a sound for training that occurs at the earliest developmental age by normal children.

The rationale for this method of selection is that if a sound is acquired at an earlier age, it should be easier to teach than a later developing sound. It is interesting to note that in spite of the lack of empirical support, this rationale has been routinely adopted by many speech pathologists.

Often the clinician will select for training a sound the child can produce as a result of imitation or minor instruction. This concept is referred to as *stimulability*. The rationale for utilizing stimulability in sound selection is that articulation therapy should require less time if the child is already able to produce the target sound with minor instruction (stimulable). Consistency is a factor related to stimulability. It is often assumed that if a sound is inconsistently misarticulated, it will be easier to correct than a sound consistently misarticulated. Another related factor is the extent to which the correction of the sound is amenable to visual clues. Many clinicians have long made the assumption that, because one could "see" the correct production of some sounds (e.g., /f/), such sounds would be easier to teach than others (e.g., /k/). One cannot help noting, however, that some frequently misarticulated sounds (e.g., /th/) have visual clues associated with them. Interesting, too, is the finding that vowels, which are less amenable to visual clues than most consonants, are acquired very early by the young child and are rarely misarticulated.

Since speech sounds are influenced by adjacent sounds, their correctness may be often related to specific phonetic contexts. This notion is often termed *coarticulation*. The production of /s/, for example, may be adequate in the word "steal" but not in "smell" because of the close proximity of the points of articulation for /s/ and /t/ in the vocal tract. Certain therapy approaches make use of the phonetic contexts. These approaches may treat a sound that is already correct in certain contexts before dealing with one that is not produced correctly in any phonetic context.

While certain misarticulations do not seem to impair intelligibility, it appears that other articulatory errors do. This reduction in intelligibility seems due to several factors, such as the number of sounds misarticulated and the types of articulatory errors made. It also appears that the frequency with which the misarticulated sound occurs in the language could also play a role. To cite an extreme example, consistent misarticulation of a rare sound would probably not constitute a problem worthy of correction, since its usage in the English language is quite limited. However, the misarticulation of /s/, a frequently used consonant in English, would be considered an articulation disorder. Therefore, it would follow that a frequently used sound might be selected for treatment rather than a less frequently used sound. Like some of the other sound selection criteria, however, the frequency-of-occurrence notion is as yet unverified empirically.

1. The author's primary purpose in this passage is to
   (A) distinguish between more important and less important sounds
   (B) define the terminology of articulation therapy
   (C) explain the criteria used in sound selection therapy
   (D) stress the empirical validity of therapeutic approaches
   (E) establish a priority ranking of articulation disorders

2. Clinicians who select a sound for training that occurs at the earliest developmental age probably reason which of the following?
   (A) Sounds occurring early are the basis of all sounds.
   (B) Sounds occurring early are the more important sounds.
   (C) Empirical support is not as persuasive as their assumptive rationale.
   (D) Sounds occurring early are probably easier to learn.
   (E) Normal children learn faster than those with articulation problems.

3. According to the passage, one distinguishing characteristic of /f/ is that
   (A) it can be heard more easily than /k/
   (B) it is acquired earlier than most vowels
   (C) very few children misarticulate it
   (D) the movements of the lips and mouth are very noticeable during pronunciation
   (E) very many children misarticulate it

4. According to the passage, those sounds selected for treatment tend to be
   (A) those which are not necessarily easy to learn
   (B) those which are frequently used in English
   (C) misarticulated by very young children only
   (D) those whose pronunciation is not influenced by their phonetic context
   (E) those which are less amenable to visual clues

5. Which of the following is a possible definition of a phonetic context?
   (A) the correctness of two or more adjacent sounds
   (B) the relationship between adjacent consonants or adjacent vowels
   (C) those adjacent sounds which stimulate the target sound
   (D) the relationship between adjacent sounds
   (E) the points of articulation in the vocal tract

6. Which of the following statements best summarizes central ideas in the passage?
   (A) A number of misarticulated sounds do not require treatment.
   (B) The selection of misarticulated sounds for treatment creates disagreement between those conducting research and those giving treatment.
   (C) The selection of misarticulated sounds for treatment depends exclusively on the stimulability and coarticulation of the sound.
   (D) The selection of misarticulated sounds for treatment depends upon empirical research verifying the assumptions of clinicians.
   (E) The selection of misarticulated sounds for treatment depends upon both the presumed difficulty of learning the sound and its frequency of occurrence.

7. The author would most likely agree with which of the following conclusions about the sound selection criteria used by clinicians?
   (A) Clinicians are easily influenced by their colleagues' selection of criteria.
   (B) Criteria should be based upon social rather than empirical factors.
   (C) Criteria do not reflect careful thinking on the part of clinicians.
   (D) Criteria change when the child's first language is not English.
   (E) Criteria are often based upon unverified rationale.

Questions 8 through 14 refer to the following passage

One of the most influential positions regarding the nature of psychology and how it can be applied to education is exemplified by the work of B. F. Skinner. Skinner's system probably represents the most complete and systematic statement of the associationist, behaviorist, environmentalist, determinist position in psychology today.

Because of his preoccupation with strict scientific controls, Skinner has performed most of his experiments with lower animals—principally the pigeon and the white rat. He developed what has become known as the "Skinner box" as a suitable device for animal study. Typically, a rat is placed in a closed box which contains only a lever and a food dispenser. When the rat presses the lever under the conditions established by the experimenter, a food pellet drops into the food tray, thus rewarding the rat. Once the rat has acquired this response, the experimenter can bring the rat's behavior under the control of a variety of stimulus conditions. Furthermore, behavior can be gradually modified or shaped until new responses not ordinarily in the rat's behavioral repertory appear. Success in these endeavors has led Skinner to believe that the laws of learning apply to all organisms. In schools the behavior of pupils may be shaped by careful sequencing of materials and by the presentation of appropriate rewards or reinforcers. Programed learning and teaching machines are the most appropriate means of accomplishing school learning. What is common to man, pigeons, and rats is a world in which certain contingencies of reinforcements prevail.

Skinner established himself as one of the country's leading behaviorists with the publication of his *Behavior of Organisms* in 1938. Although obviously influenced by Watson's behaviorism, Skinner's system appears to follow primarily from the work of Pavlov and Thorndike. Unlike some other followers of Watson, who studied behavior in order to understand the "workings of the mind," Skinner restricted himself to the study of overt or measurable behavior. Without denying either mental or physiological processes, he finds that a study of behavior does not depend on conclusions about what is going on inside the organism.

Every science, he points out, has looked for causes of action inside the things it has studied. Although the practice has proved useful at times, the problem is that events which are located inside a system are likely to be difficult to observe. We are inclined to provide inner explanations without justification, and invent causes without fear of contradiction. It is especially tempting to attribute human behavior to the behavior of some inner agent.

Because we have for so long looked inside the organism for an explanation of behavior, we have neglected the variables which are immediately available for a scientific analysis. These variables lie outside the organism. They are found in its immediate environment or in its environmental history. Many of the variables or stimuli are measurable and controllable and, consequently, they make it possible to explain behavior as other subjects are explained in science.

It is evident that the methods of science have been highly successful. Skinner believes that the methods of science should be applied to the field of human affairs. We are all controlled by the world, part of which is constructed by men. Is this control to occur by accident, by tyrants, or by ourselves? A scientific society should reject accidental manipulation. He asserts that a specific plan is needed to promote fully the development of man and society. We cannot make wise decisions if we continue to pretend that we are not controlled.

As Skinner points out, the possibility of behavioral control is offensive to many people. We have traditionally regarded man as a free agent whose behavior occurs by virtue of spontaneous inner changes. We are reluctant to abandon the internal "will" which makes prediction and control of behavior impossible.

8. According to the passage, Skinner would agree with each of the following statements *except*
   (A) rats and pigeons are appropriate animals for behavioristic study
   (B) these behaviors we normally exhibit are not the only ones we are capable of
   (C) the concept of behavioral control has popular appeal
   (D) inner causes of behavior are more difficult to observe than outer ones
   (E) positive reinforcement will affect learning in school

9. The author implies that Skinner feels that the scientific procedure he advocates might be effective as
   (A) a political procedure
   (B) an explanation of the causes of dictatorships
   (C) a means for replacing teachers with computers
   (D) a way of identifying characteristics common to rats, pigeons, and humans
   (E) a way to understand the human mind

10. Which of the following statements would most appropriately continue the paragraph at the end of the passage?
    (A) The offensive qualities of Skinner's theory make serious attention to it almost impossible.
    (B) But the scientific method has shown us that behavior can be predicted; so we are in a quandary.
    (C) Skinner simply denies the existence of internal personality factors.
    (D) And so Skinner's theory is replaced by the more rational voice of popular opinion.
    (E) All those who question Skinner's theory are, simply, wrong.

11. Which of the following statements would most weaken Skinner's theory as described by the author?
    (A) New research shows that the mind is even more complicated than had been supposed.
    (B) Skinner's experiments are always careful and precise.
    (C) The number of rats and pigeons available for research is decreasing.
    (D) Certain human traits are similar to those of rats and pigeons.
    (E) Modern technology has discovered methods of measuring the internal workings of the mind.

12. We may infer which of the following about Watson's behaviorism?
    (A) It has partially influenced Skinner's work.
    (B) It preceded and preempted Skinner's work.
    (C) It was identical to Skinner's work.
    (D) It has focused on the inner workings of the mind.
    (E) It paid far too much attention to the internal behavior of organisms.

13. We may infer which of the following about the "Skinner box"?
   (A) It can be adapted for the controlled study of all organisms.
   (B) It represents a stimulus-response relationship similar to such relationships in the more complex human world.
   (C) It has been designed with the recognition that rats prefer enclosed places.
   (D) It allows a study of the relationship between rats and pigeons.
   (E) It was used for scientific research before Skinner began his own studies.

14. The author of the passage answers all of the following questions *except*
   (A) do Skinnerians deny that mental and physiological processes exist?
   (B) is Skinner's work relevant to education?
   (C) are lower animals easier to study than higher ones?
   (D) has Skinner been influenced by Pavlov?
   (E) has Skinner's behaviorism been applied to the control of human society?

Questions 15 through 21 refer to the following passage

In economics, demand implies something slightly different from the common meaning of the term. The layman, for example, often uses the term to mean the amount that is demanded of an item. Thus, if the price were to decrease and individuals wanted more of the item, it is commonly said that demand increases. To an economist, demand is a relationship between a series of prices and a series of corresponding quantities that are demanded at these prices. If one reads the previous sentences carefully, it should become apparent that there is a distinction between the quantity demanded and demand. This distinction is often a point of confusion and we all should be aware of and understand the difference between these two terms. We repeat, therefore, that demand is a relationship between price and quantities demanded, and therefore suggests the effect of one (e.g., price) on the other (e.g., quantity demanded).

Therefore, knowledge of the demand for a product enables one to predict how much more of a good will be purchased if price decreases. But the increase in quantity demanded does not mean demand has increased, since the relationship between price and quantity demanded (i.e., the demand for the product) has not changed. Demand shifts when there is a change in income, expectations, taste, etc., such that a different quantity of the good is demanded at the same price.

In almost all cases, a consumer wants more of an item if the price decreases. This relationship between price and quantity demanded is so strong that it is referred to as the "law of demand." This "law" can be explained by the income and substitution effects. The income effect occurs because price increases reduce the purchasing power of the individual and, thus, the quantity demanded of goods must decrease. The substitution effect reflects the consumer's desire to get the "best buy." Accordingly, if the price of good A increases, the individual will tend to substitute another good and purchase less of good A. The negative correlation between price and quantity demanded is also explained by the law of diminishing marginal utility. According to this law, the additional utility the consumer gains from consuming a good decreases as successively more units of the good are consumed. Because the additional units yield less utility or satisfaction, the consumer is willing to purchase more only if the price of the good decreases.

Economists distinguish between individual and market demand. As the term implies, individual demand concerns the individual consumer and illustrates the quantities that individuals demand at different prices. Market demand includes the demand of all individuals for a particular good and is found by summing the quantities demanded by all individuals at the various prices.

The other side of the price system is supply. As in the case of demand, supply is a relationship between a series of prices and the associated quantities supplied. It is assumed that as price increases the individual or firm will supply greater quantities of a good. There is a positive correlation between quantity supplied and product price.

Economists also distinguish between a change in supply and quantity supplied. The distinction is similar to the one made with respect to demand. Also, as in the case of demand, economists distinguish between individual firm supply and market supply, which is the summation of individual supply.

Taken together, supply and demand yield equilibrium prices and quantity. Equilibrium is a state of stability, with balanced forces in which prices and quantity will remain constant. Moreover, there are forces in the market that will act to establish equilibrium if changes in demand or supply create disequilibrium. For example, if prices are above equilibrium, the quantity supplied exceeds quantity demanded and surpluses occur that have a downward pressure on prices. These pressures will persist until equilibrium is established. If prices are below equilibrium, the good will become scarce and there will be an upward pressure on price.

In reality, equilibrium is seldom attained, for the factors affecting the market are constantly changing. In a dynamic market of this kind, there is a continual process of adjustment as the market searches or gropes for equilibrium. The rapidity of adjustment will depend to a large extent on the quality of information that is available to firms and consumers.

Through the market interaction of demand and supply, a "market price" is established. This price serves two very important roles of rationing and allocating goods. Since wants far exceed resources, there must be a device by which to determine who gets the goods. In the market system, price plays this rationing role by supplying goods to all who pay the price of the product. As an allocator of goods, price insures that resources are utilized in their most valuable uses. In short, in a market system, price serves both a demand-inhibiting and a supply-eliciting function. Naturally, the market system does not work perfectly.

In most economies, the government plays a role in the market system. Governments enforce the "rules of the game," impose taxes, and may control prices through price ceilings or price supports. These actions necessarily may create shortages or surpluses. In most developed and interdependent economies, the necessity of the government playing some role in the economy seldom is disputed.

15. Assume that firms develop an orange-flavored breakfast drink high in vitamin C that is a good substitute for orange juice but sells for less. Based upon assertions in the passage, which of the following would occur with respect to the demand for orange juice?
    (A) Health food stores would resurrect the law of diminishing marginal utility.
    (B) Assuming that the price of fresh orange juice remained constant, more orange juice would be consumed.
    (C) The law of demand would prevail.
    (D) Assuming that the price of fresh orange juice remained constant, the demand would not change.
    (E) There is not enough information in the passage to answer this question.

16. According to the passage, a group of individuals will
    (A) derive less satisfaction from a product
    (B) exert individual demand under appropriate conditions
    (C) shift the demand line to the right
    (D) constitute a market
    (E) emphasize supply over demand

17. According to the passage, a change in demand would occur in which of the following situations?
    (A) The gasoline price increases, resulting in the increased sale of Datsuns (whose price remains stable).
    (B) The gasoline price increases, resulting in the increased sale of Datsuns (which go on sale in response to increased gas prices).
    (C) The gasoline price decreases on the same day that a new 43-mpg car enters the market.
    (D) A federal order imposes a price ceiling on gasoline.
    (E) A federal order lifts price regulations for gasoline.

18. According to the passage, quantity supplied and product price are not
    (A) correlative   (D) symbiotic
    (B) disjunctive   (E) consequential
    (C) related

19. Assume that the demand for houses increases. Drawing from the passage, decide which of the following would most likely cause such a shift.
    (A) Interest rates on mortgages increase.
    (B) The government predicts a large increase in the extent of unemployment.
    (C) In a poverty area, a new government program provides jobs for all who need them.
    (D) A low-priced type of mobile home is announced which is a good substitute for houses.
    (E) The cost of lumber increases.

20. The final sentence in the passage hints that
    (A) interdependence goes hand in hand with development
    (B) there are underdeveloped countries whose attitude toward government control may be hostile
    (C) disputes over government control usually come from an illiterate populace
    (D) socialism is a sophisticated achievement
    (E) capitalism is a sophisticated achievement

21. According to the final paragraph, the government's intervention in the economy may cause
    (A) higher prices
    (B) disequilibrium
    (C) lower prices
    (D) the market to tend toward socialism
    (E) the market to tend toward capitalism

Questions 22 through 28 refer to the following passage

"There is no security"—to quote his own words—"against the ultimate development of mechanical consciousness, in the fact of machines possessing little consciousness now. A mollusc has not much consciousness. Reflect upon the extraordinary advance which the machines have made during the last few hundred years, and note how slowly the animal and vegetable kingdoms are advancing in comparison. The more highly organised machines are creatures not so much of yesterday as of the last five minutes, so to speak, in comparison with past time. Assume for the sake of argument that conscious beings have existed for some twenty million years: see what strides machines have made in the last thousand! May not the world last twenty million years longer? If so, what will they not in the end become? Is it not safer to nip the mischief in the bud and to forbid them further progress?"

"But who can say that the vapour engine has not a kind of consciousness? Where does consciousness begin, and where end? Who can draw the line? Who can draw any line? Is not everything interwoven with everything? Is not machinery linked with animal life in an infinite variety of ways? The shell of a hen's egg is a machine as much as an egg-cup is: the shell is a plan for holding the egg as much as the egg-cup for holding the shell: both are phases of the same function; the hen makes the shell in her inside, but it is pure pottery. She makes her nest outside of herself for convenience' sake, but the nest is not more of a machine than the egg-shell is. A 'machine' is only a 'device.' "

. . . "Even a potato in a dark cellar has a certain low cunning about him which serves him in excellent stead. He knows perfectly well what he wants and how to get it. He sees the light coming from the cellar window and sends his shoots crawling straight thereto: they will crawl along the floor and up the wall and out at the cellar window; if there be a little earth anywhere on the journey he will find it and use it for his own ends. What deliberation he may exercise in the matter of his roots when he is planted in the earth is a thing unknown to us, but we can imagine him saying, 'I will have a tuber and a tuber there, and I will suck whatsoever advantage I can from all my surroundings. This neighbour I will overshadow, and that I will undermine; and what I can do shall be the limits of what I will do. He that is stronger and better placed than I shall overcome me, and him that is weaker I will overcome.' The potato says these things by doing them, which is the best of language. What is consciousness if this is not consciousness? We find it difficult to sympathise with the emotions of a potato; so we do with those of an oyster. Neither of these things makes a noise on being boiled or opened, and noise appeals to us more strongly than anything else, because we make so much about our own sufferings. Since then they do not annoy us by any expression of pain we call them emotionless; and so *qua* mankind they are; but mankind is not everybody."

. . ."*Either*," he proceeds, "a great deal of action that has been called purely mechanical and unconscious must be admitted to contain more elements of consciousness than has been allowed hitherto (and in this case germs of consciousness will be found in many actions of the higher machines)—*Or* (assuming the theory of evolution but at the same time denying the consciousness of vegetable and crystalline action) the race of man has descended from things which had no consciousness at all. In this case there is no *a priori* improbability in the descent of conscious (and more than conscious) machines from those which now exist, except that which is suggested by the apparent absence of anything like a reproductive system in the mechanical kingdom."

22. When the speaker uses *qua* at the conclusion of the third paragraph, he probably means
   (A) against
   (B) compared to
   (C) as well as
   (D) with the help of
   (E) unaffected by

23. We can conclude that the author of this passage
   (A) believes that certain plants may display the characteristics of consciousness
   (B) believes that the consciousness of machines is comparable to the consciousness of humans
   (C) is not the same as the speaker, and therefore may not share any of the speaker's views
   (D) is writing this passage amidst the twentieth-century boom in high technology
   (E) holds that machines cannot reproduce themselves

24. The primary purpose of this speaker is to
    (A) argue that machines and other presumably unconscious things do possess a sort of consciousness
    (B) describe the widespread proliferation of machines and the effects of it
    (C) ridicule those who have not thought deeply about the relationship between consciousness and lack of consciousness
    (D) show that creatures may be both cunning and silent
    (E) express fear that the machine age may displace human, animal, and plant life

25. The main argument of the passage is summarized in which of the following places?
    (A) the first sentence of the first paragraph
    (B) the first sentence of the second paragraph
    (C) the first sentence of the third paragraph
    (D) the first sentence of the fourth paragraph
    (E) the last sentence of the third paragraph

26. From the second paragraph we may infer the speaker's belief that
    (A) the vapour engine thinks for itself
    (B) mechanical life and animal life are mirror images of each other
    (C) nothing is certain
    (D) the creation of egg cups was as natural as the creation of eggs
    (E) the world is a system of interrelationships

27. From the speaker we may infer which of the following conclusions about silent creatures such as potatoes and oysters?
    (A) They do not suffer.
    (B) They have feelings.
    (C) Their behavior is well known to the author.
    (D) They do not speak because speaking is not the best of languages.
    (E) They are not related to mankind.

28. The speaker implies that one of the causes of the limited human understanding of consciousness and lack of consciousness is

(A) the fact that humans descended from things which never had any consciousness at all

(B) the unlikelihood that any human has ever listened to a potato

(C) the human tendency to characterize other creatures with reference only to human characteristics

(D) the human avoidance of machines that are able to think

(E) the breach of security which occurs when machines, which are presumably amoral, take over many of the moral duties of advanced society

STOP. IF YOU FINISH BEFORE TIME IS CALLED, CHECK YOUR WORK ON THIS SECTION ONLY. DO NOT WORK ON ANY OTHER SECTION IN THE TEST.

ANSWER KEY FOR PRACTICE TEST 1

Section I Reading Comprehension		Section II Analytical Reasoning		Section III Dispute Characterization			
1. D		1. B		1. D		21. D	
2. B		2. D		2. A		22. B	
3. C		3. D		3. C		23. A	
4. E		4. E		4. C		24. B	
5. E		5. C		5. B		25. B	
6. B		6. B		6. D		26. D	
7. D		7. E		7. D		27. C	
8. A		8. B		8. B		28. C	
9. C		9. B		9. A		29. A	
10. E		10. E		10. D		30. B	
11. B		11. D		11. C		31. A	
12. C		12. A		12. C		32. B	
13. E		13. E		13. B		33. C	
14. A		14. C		14. B		34. D	
15. D		15. B		15. C		35. B	
16. C		16. C		16. A		36. C	
17. C		17. C		17. D		37. D	
18. E		18. E		18. C		38. A	
19. C		19. E		19. B		39. C	
20. C		20. C		20. C		40. B	
21. B		21. E					
22. D		22. A					
23. C		23. E					
24. B		24. D					
25. A		25. E					
26. B		26. C					
27. B							

ANSWER KEY FOR PRACTICE TEST 1

Section IV Logical Reasoning	Section V Analytical Reasoning	Section VI Reading Comprehension
1. C	1. C	1. C
2. E	2. D	2. D
3. D	3. C	3. D
4. C	4. D	4. B
5. E	5. A	5. D
6. A	6. D	6. E
7. D	7. C	7. E
8. E	8. D	8. C
9. A	9. A	9. A
10. C	10. C	10. B
11. B	11. B	11. E
12. E	12. E	12. A
13. E	13. C	13. B
14. A	14. D	14. E
15. C	15. D	15. C
16. A	16. A	16. D
17. E	17. E	17. A
18. D	18. D	18. B
19. D	19. C	19. C
20. D	20. A	20. B
21. D	21. D	21. B
22. C	22. B	22. B
23. C	23. E	23. C
24. D	24. A	24. A
25. D	25. E	25. D
26. C	26. B	26. E
		27. B
		28. C

HOW TO SCORE YOUR EXAM

Your score on the actual LSAT is simply the number of questions you answered correctly (minus a small adjustment factor) scaled to a 10–48 scoring range. There is no penalty for incorrect answers other than no credit.

ANALYZING YOUR TEST RESULTS

The charts on the following pages should be used to carefully analyze your results and spot your strengths and weaknesses. The complete process of analyzing each subject area and each individual problem should be completed for each Practice Test. These results should then be reexamined for trends in types of errors (repeated errors) or poor results in specific subject areas. THIS REEXAMINATION AND ANALYSIS IS VERY IMPORTANT TO YOU: IT SHOULD ENABLE YOU TO CONCENTRATE ON YOUR AREAS OF WEAKNESS.

PRACTICE TEST 1: ANALYSIS SHEET

	Possible	Completed	Right	Wrong
Section I: Reading Comprehension	27			
Section II: Analytical Reasoning	26			
Section III: Dispute Characterization	40			
Section IV: Logical Reasoning	26			
Section V: Analytical Reasoning	26			
Section VI: Reading Comprehension	28			
OVERALL TOTALS	173			

WHY??????????????????????????????????

ANALYSIS—TALLY SHEET FOR PROBLEMS MISSED

One of the most important parts of test preparation is analyzing why you missed a problem so that you can reduce the number of future mistakes. Now that you have taken Practice Test 1 and corrected your answers, carefully tally your mistakes by marking them in the proper column.

	REASON FOR MISTAKE			
	Total Missed	Simple Mistake	Misread Problem	Lack of Knowledge
Section I: Reading Comprehension				
Section II: Analytical Reasoning				
Section III: Dispute Characterization				
Section IV: Logical Reasoning				
Section V: Analytical Reasoning				
Section VI: Reading Comprehension				
OVERALL TOTALS				

Reviewing the above data should help you determine WHY you are missing certain problems. Now that you have pinpointed the type of error, take the next practice test and focus on avoiding your most common type.

ANSWERS AND COMPLETE EXPLANATIONS FOR PRACTICE TEST 1

SECTION I: READING COMPREHENSION

1. (D) The first paragraph implies the importance of articulation disorders by mentioning how heavily they contribute to a clinician's caseload.

2. (B) In the second paragraph, functional disorders are compared in general with organic disorders. Each of the other choices is too specific to apply to *any* articulation disorder.

3. (C) Although the author does not flatly argue against the treatment of articulation disorders, he or she repeatedly gives reasons that treatment may not be necessary; because the author is not convinced of the necessity for treatment, we may term the attitude skeptical.

4. (E) This is explicitly stated at the end of paragraph 3; all other choices are statements with which the author implicitly or explicitly *dis*agrees.

5. (E) Choice (A) is too general, and (B), (C), and (D) are too specific, referring to only portions of the passage. In terms of both causes and treatments, the author consistently discusses controversial (not clearly resolved) points of view.

6. (B) The need to develop more efficient procedures is mentioned in the final paragraph and is connected with the issue of accountability and the fact that children may overcome the disorder with or without treatment. Thus, treatment that aids children in overcoming the disorder more quickly than they might without treatment becomes important.

7. (D) The rest of the sentence indicates that the studies were conducted over several years; no other meaning of *longitudinal* is expressed or implied in the sentence.

8. (A) Phrases such as "A basic concept for student awareness . . ." and "It is important for students to realize . . ." imply that the author is writing for an audience of students.

9. (C) In the fifth paragraph, the author calls this translation into question by suggesting the many possible meanings of *euthanasia.*

10. (E) In the second paragraph, the author discusses two developments that have contributed to the importance of euthanasia; choice (E) reiterates the second development discussed. Each of the other choices mentions a subject touched upon in the passage, but none of these subjects is connected so explicitly with the importance of euthanasia as a social issue.

11. (B) Although the essay offers implied and expressed arguments for and against the legality of euthanasia, the author remains indefinite about whether it should be legalized or whether practitioners should be punished. Paragraph 5 suggests that suicide can be considered a type of euthanasia, but that possibility is rejected in the following paragraph defining the term literally; the relationship between suicide and euthanasia remains ambiguous.

12. (C) The passage is a general summary which contains arguments but which of itself does not constitute one; therefore (A) and (B) are weak choices. (D) and (E) are both too narrow, stressing secondary rather than primary purposes of the passage.

13. (E) The unchanging "official" attitude toward euthanasia is compared with the changing attitude toward the death penalty. Choices (A), (B), and (C) may refer to euthanasia in particular, but not to capital punishment. Choice (D) is not suggested in any way.

14. (A) The passage asserts that the growing importance of euthanasia as a social and moral issue has partially resulted from the growth of advanced technology and coincident medical advances. Therefore, we may infer that euthanasia has not become as important an issue in less advanced regions.

15. (D) *Evolution* is to *species* in the same way as *bush* is to *branches.* Just as the branches of a bush reach out every which way in varying lengths, the results of evolution (forms of life; species) have developed in irregular "branches." This is the main point of paragraph 2.

16. (C) A "predecessor" is that which comes before. Since, according to paragraph 1, "nucleosides produced nucleotides," *nucleosides* came before (are predecessors of) *nucleic acids.*

17. (C) Paragraph 3 states that "cotylosaurs, branched into the unsuccessful dinosaurs and . . . the successful turtles."

18. (E) The New World usually refers to America (North *and* South America). Since no monkeys are native to North America, as most Americans should know, New World monkeys must inhabit South America.

19. (C) The first paragraph lists water, hydrogen, ammonia, and hydrogen cyanide as the only members of the primordial mixture.

20. (C) "The Failure of Tax Reform" is briefly implied only in the first sentence of paragraph 2. And "The Prevalence of *Koine*" is the topic of only one sentence in Paragraph 3. So all choices which contain these titles (B, D, E) are incorrect. In choice (A), "Patriarchs vs. the Pope" is inaccurate.

21. (B) *There* directly follows *Western counterpart;* this positioning suggests that *there* refers to the Western Empire.

22. (D) This answer is implied by facts in the first paragraph: (1) the inhabitants of the Eastern Empire still called themselves Romans; (2) "a large bureaucracy [was] inherited from the Roman Empire." And in the second paragraph, Justinian's laws are compared with the preceding Roman laws.

23. (C) This answer is supported by paragraph 3, which mentions several reasons for infanticide; in general, each infanticide is justified insofar as the birth is unfortunate for the society as a whole. In all cases infanticide is "a technique of population control." (A) is a possible choice, but the religious implications of infanticide are more implicit than explicit in the passage.

24. (B) Paragraph 7 abruptly leaves the topic of birth and childhood and concentrates on age and death. A transitional sentence would be useful for eliminating such abruptness. (A) is inconsistent with the form of the passage; there are no subtitles anywhere. (C) would call for information which may or may not be relevant at that point. (D) would be out of place and useless insofar as it supplies definitions long *after* the words have been used. (E) is inconsistent with the author's straightforward, nonopinionated presentation.

25. (A) This is true of Oceania, which in some parts requires a woman "to give proof that she is fertile before she is permitted to

marry." She could give such proof only by becoming pregnant; menstruation (C) is not itself proof of fertility.

26. (B) The passage states that infanticide is used in many societies "as a technique of population control." Only (B) is such a technique although (A) may control population without meaning to. (C) refers to an economic, rather than psychological, phenomenon.

27. (B) Near the end of the passage, burial in the fetal position is mentioned. So a connection is suggested between the fetus (unborn child) and the corpse, between birth and death.

SECTION II: ANALYTICAL REASONING

To construct your chart for questions 1 to 7, it may be easiest to list the letters A, B, C, and D consecutively, leaving room between them to place in numbers. Your chart should then have looked like this:

4 6 A 5 B 2 C 1 D 3   or   4 6 A 5 B 2 C 3 D 1

1. (B) B is between 1 and A, but *not* next to either.

2. (D) Both I and II must be true.

3. (D) If 3 is the last figure, then 1 is before D, which puts it next to C.

4. (E) The numbers next to B are 2 and 5, which total to 7.

5. (C) To add two more letters to the list, they must go after D to stay in alphabetical order. But then they don't have a number between them to abide by the rules. Thus, the answer is (C).

6. (B) B is the fifth position. The nearest other letters are third and seventh.

7. (E) The first two numbers in the list total 10, which is twice 5 and greater than the total of the last three numbers, 6.

8. (B) II is true. Since four of the six children have blue eyes and three of the six are girls, then at least one girl has blue eyes. All of the girls do not have to have freckles.

9. (B) II must be false. Since five of the six children have freckles and four of the six children have blue eyes, then some of the freckled children must have blue eyes. Statement I, "all the blue-eyed girls have freckles," could be true.

10. (E) None of the statements can be deduced from the information given.

11. (D) "Three children have brown eyes" must be false. Since four children have blue eyes, that would total seven children. There are only six children in the family.

For questions 12 to 17, constructing a chart would be helpful.

	A	B	C	D	F
Rich	A	—	—	—	—
Ron	—	—	C	—	—
Holly	—	?	—	?	—
Maria	—	—	—	—	F
Sheila	—	?	—	?	—

Use the given information as follows to complete this elimination chart.

If Maria gets a lower grade than Holly, then Maria can't get an A and Holly can't get an F.

If Holly gets a lower grade than Rich, then Holly can't get an A and Rich can't get an F.

Ron and Sheila do not get F's; therefore, you can deduce that Maria gets the F.

If Maria gets the F, she can receive no other grade.

If Rich gets the top grade, an A, then he can get no other grade and no one else can get an A.

Ron's grade is halfway between Maria's and Rich's and is therefore a C.

This leaves Holly and Sheila; one gets a B and the other a D, but we do not know who gets which.

12. (A) Statement I must be true, since Rich gets the A, but we do not know whether Sheila gets a B or a D.

13. (E) Statement I must be true, since Rich gets an A. Statement II is true based on the information in the chart. Therefore, neither must be false.

14. (C) From the chart, it is evident that a comparison between Sheila's grade and Holly's grade cannot be made.

15. (B) The information in the chart tells us that if Holly gets a B, then Sheila gets a D.

16. (C) From the chart we know that Sheila cannot get a C because Ron does and Maria gets an F. So both statements are true.

17. (C) Sheila's getting a B means that Holly must get a D. This is evident from the chart.

18. (E) From the information given, you may deduce that Holly received the B or the D and that Sheila received the D or the B. However, you cannot determine who received which.

19. (E) Since Ron got the C and Holly got either a B or a D, then for Tom's grade to be between Ron's and Holly's, Tom must have gotten either a B−, a C+, a C−, or a D+.

For questions 20 to 26 you may have constructed a chart.

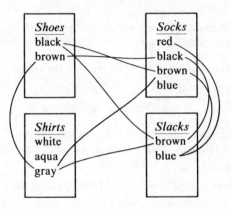

20. (C) Black does not go well with brown.

21. (E) Statements II and III are true, since black does not go well with brown and blue socks may be worn with brown slacks.

22. (A) Blue slacks cannot be worn with red socks.

23. (E) There are 48 possible combinations. 4 socks × 3 shirts × 2 slacks × 2 shoes.

24. (D) Statements I, II, and III are true. Sam could wear a white shirt, brown slacks, and blue socks. The only general statement is that black does not go with brown.

25. (E) Statements I, II, and III are true. Red socks may not be worn with blue slacks, and brown doesn't go with black. Also, brown socks cannot be worn with blue slacks. Therefore he must wear blue socks.

26. (C) All the other combinations are prohibited.

SECTION III: DISPUTE CHARACTERIZATION

Set 1

1. (D) This question is irrelevant. The length of the fence had absolutely no bearing on the dispute and is not mentioned in either of the rules.

2. (A) This is a relevant question which, based on the facts in the question, would lead to different answers depending upon which rule is chosen. By Rule I Nugget would win the suit; by Rule II Acorn would win. There is no reason to use one rule over the other. Thus this question requires a choice between the rules.

3. (C) Both rules lead to the same answer to this relevant question. In each case Acorn would win the suit.

4. (C) This is a relevant question having bearing on the dispute. It is easily answered by the facts of the case.

5. (B) This relevant question requires additional information to be answered—that is, information about liability of leasers.

6. (D) This question is irrelevant. The reasons that the slide and pool were restricted to private use are not essential to the dispute as governed by these rules.

Set 2

7. (D) This is an irrelevant question. The cost of the advertisements has no bearing on the dispute.

8. (B) This is a relevant question; if Earthfood can substantiate its written claims, by Rule I they are not guilty. To answer this question, however, additional facts are necessary.

9. (A) This is a relevant question. If the representation was false, but not intentional, then by Rule I Earthfood is guilty. But if the representation is false, but not intentional, then by Rule II Earthfood is *not* guilty. There is no reason to use one rule over another. Therefore a choice is necessary.

10. (D) The success of the advertising has no bearing on the outcome of the dispute. Therefore this relevant question can be answered.

11. (C) If the Earthfood case is false and intentional, Earthfood will be found guilty by both rules. Therefore this relevant question can be answered.

12. (C) If the Earthfood claim was true and could be substantiated by factual data, Earthfood will be found not guilty by both rules. Therefore this relevant question can also be answered.

Set 3

13. (B) A previous stipulation is an important part of Rule I, and thus this is a relevant question. Whether there was such a previous stipulation regarding liabilities is not stated in the facts. Thus additional information is needed to answer the question.

14. (B) The cost of the damages is an important factor for Rule II, and thus this is a relevant question. Here, too, the information to answer this question is not contained in the facts of the case. More facts are necessary.

15. (C) This relevant question can be answered by applying Rule I; the contractee is not liable and thus will not pay Sal. Rule II does not apply, since the damages were not over $300.

16. (A) Each of the rules yields a different outcome. By Rule I the contractee (Brian) is not liable. But by Rule II Brian is liable, since the damages were over $300. Since there is no reason to use one rule over the other, a choice is necessary.

17. (D) The fee for painting is irrelevant to the outcome of the dispute as governed by the rules.

18. (C) Both rules give the same answer to this relevant question. By Rule I Brian will pay Sal because spilling turpentine was not an ordinary circumstance. By Rule II Brian will also have to pay Sal because the damages were over $300.

Set 4

19. (B) By the facts it is unclear whether Frank was aware during or after the transaction that the television had been stolen. By Rule I he would have to know of the stolen status as he purchased to be guilty of larceny. We do not know when he was told by the seller. More facts are necessary. Rule II does not apply.

20. (C) This relevant question is answerable by the facts. If Frank was informed after he purchased the television that it was stolen property, by Rule I he is not guilty of larceny. Likewise, by Rule II, his having returned the television to the police ensures that he is not guilty of a crime.

21. (D) The value of the television has no bearing on the outcome of the case. This is an irrelevant question.

22. (B) As in question 19, *when* Frank was told about the stolen television is crucial to Rule I. Here, again, more information is needed.

23. (A) If Frank had known *before* he bought the television that it was stolen, by Rule I he is guilty of larceny. However, since he returned it to the police, by Rule II he would not be guilty. Since there is no reason to use one rule over the other, a choice is necessary between the rules.

Set 5

24. (B) To answer this relevant question, we need additional information. Rule II does not apply, since the call was made after three days, but we do not know if Rule I applies. We do not know if the agreement was in writing.

25. (B) To answer this relevant question, we need a definition or clarification of "adequate cause."

26. (D) This question is irrelevant.

27. (C) This relevant question can be easily answered by the facts. No, he went to another company and had the pool installed. This information is important to the application of Rule II.

28. (C) This relevant question can be readily answered, as both rules lead us to the same answer. Yes, Pennypincher will win the suit.

29. (A) To answer this relevant question, we must choose between the rules. By Rule I the contract could not be terminated because there was not adequate cause to do so. By Rule II the contract could be voided within the legal time limit.

Set 6

30. (B) This is a relevant question that has important bearing on the dispute. If Bill was, in fact, temporarily insane, by Rule I he is not guilty; whereas by Rule II he would be. Thus it is essential to determine "temporary insanity." Since neither the facts nor the rules clarify "temporary insanity" enough to make a judgment, more facts are needed.

31. (A) This relevant question is answered differently by each of the rules. By Rule I Bill is not guilty. By Rule II he is guilty. Since there is no reason to use one rule over the other, a choice is necessary.

32. (B) Since "comprehension of the severity of his or her actions" is an essential criterion of temporary insanity in Rule II, this is a relevant question. However it requires more facts in order to be answered, as we do not know if Bill was aware of the effect of his actions.

33. (C) This relevant question is answered the same way by either rule. In both cases Bill would be found guilty.

34. (D) The degree of damage to the television is irrelevant. There was damage; how much is beside the point.

Set 7

35. (B) This is a relevant question because negligence is the important issue in Rule II. Whether Mike was indeed negligent is uncertain. Additional facts are necessary.

36. (C) This relevant question is easily answered by the rules. By Rule I Mike will win the suit because Nan caused the damages by breaking the law. By Rule II Mike will, again, win the suit because he was not negligent in packing; rather, Nan was negligent in not observing the stop sign.

37. (D) This question is irrelevant. The effectiveness of the four-way stop is unimportant and has no bearing on the outcome of the dispute.

38. (A) This relevant question requires a choice between the rules. By Rule I Nan still broke the law and would lose the suit. By Rule II Mike was negligent, so Nan would win the suit. There is no reason to use one rule over the other, and each rule yields a different result.

39. (C) This is a relevant question because the issue of damages is central to the dispute: if there were no damages, there would be no dispute. And the question is easily answerable by the facts: yes, there were damages because six glass lamps were broken.

40. (B) This is a relevant question having important bearing on Rule I. If Mike did not stop at the stop sign, he is liable by Rule I. But whether he stopped is not stated by the facts of the case. Therefore more information is necessary.

SECTION IV: LOGICAL REASONING

1. (C) The transitional word *nevertheless* establishes a juxtaposition of the phrases immediately before and after it. Therefore (A) and (B) are incorrect. Choice (D) may be a good answer, but (C) is better, as it addresses a concern initially introduced in the paragraph and brings the passage full circle.

2. (E) Only (C) and (E) describe situations in which a media event precedes a real-life event. In (C) the medium is not an artistic one; in (E) television may be regarded as an art form.

3. (D) Choices (B) and (E) are contradicted by the passage, and the passage does not support the probability of (A) or (C). Choice (D) is reasonable, plausible, and probable, given the information in the passage.

4. (C) The student's qualification shows that he or she doubts whether the Congressman's statement is absolutely true, but the response is not so pronounced as to suggest any of the other choices.

5. (E) The passage restricts its attention to salaries, and its details clearly indicate that federal pay is significantly high, thus possibly supporting the conclusion in (E).

6. (A) This statement is consistent with the comparison between federal and private workers established in the passage. Choice (D) contradicts information in the passage, (C) is irrelevant, and (B) and (E) are not mentioned in the passage.

7. (D) The argument presupposes both that candidates are spending too much on television advertising ("the waste") and that television can be used to inform the public ("provide air time to all candidates to debate the issues"). Statement III is irrelevant to the argument.

8. (E) This choice weakens the point made by the final observation. Each of the other choices either strengthen points made by the observation or are irrelevant.

9. (A) Only this choice necessarily introduces a contrasting statement, one which would probably take issue with the points of the argument. (C) and (D) might possibly begin critical, contrasting statements but may have other uses as well.

10. (C) Geographic location and employment status are irrelevant issues, so (A) and (B) should be eliminated. (D) and (E) are too general and vague. Only (C) makes explicit the point of the author's argument, that interpretation of the Texas law is arrogant and unsound.

11. (B) By describing the special relief programs as a "flood," the author gives the programs a negative connotation and suggests disapproval.

12. (E) The researcher concluded that women could be just as capable as men in math but that they develop other abilities because of social pressures. Thus, the researcher assumes that women do conform to social expectations.

13. (E) Choices (A) and (B) are irrelevant to the argument, and (D) is an illogical criticism. (E) is a logical conclusion that poses a significant problem.

14. (A) All of the other choices are much less relevant than the issue of how efficiently and effectively the program helps students to achieve competency.

15. (C) Each of the other choices requires assumptions and conclusions not supported or implied by the argument. The stress in the argument on reduced funds leads logically to the conclusion that further spending is unwise.

16. (A) Bacon advocates retaining dignity without intruding upon liberty. The author implies that retaining dignity is impossible without intruding upon another's liberty by stating that not intruding upon liberty is impossible. (B), (C), and (D) contradict the author's argument, and (E) presents an irrelevant issue.

17. (E) I and II only. The author both relies on an interpretation of Bacon's statement and discusses liberty and dignity in absolute terms; I and II subvert such reliance. III supports, reiterates in fact, the author's argument.

18. (D) Jonathan Swift is comparing laws to a cobweb, noting that little insects get caught but big insects can break on through. He thus is indicating that the legal system is inequitable: that the "small" will get caught (sentenced) while those with more power can avoid sentencing.

19. (D) The passage sets up the thesis that sometimes individuals yield to others' interests. Choices (A) and (E) are unsubstantiated or not mentioned in the passage; (C) does not fit the structure of the sentence; (B) could possibly be the correct answer, but (D) more nearly completes the thought of the passage and is neatly juxtaposed with the first part of the incomplete sentence.

20. (D) The author does not address the distinction between how much sleep we desire and how much our bodies require. Each of the other distinctions is addressed in the passage.

21. (D) In the passage, becoming older corresponds with "*advanced* knowledge and capabilities." Choices (A), (B), and (C) should be eliminated because each is contradicted by the assumptions of the passage (the passage suggests that *more* sleep is undesirable, knowledge and capabilities are connected with *wakefulness,* and mindlessness is connected with *sleep*). Choice (E) is a generalization not at all concerned with amount of sleep and therefore not relevant to the passage.

22. (C) Choices (A), (B), and (E) present information that supports the value of sleep, and (D) dissociates advanced capabilities from the mind, thus damaging the author's mind/mindlessness distinction.

23. (C) Only choice (C) asserts the positive value of sleep and thus weakens the author's stance in favor of decreased sleep.

24. (D) The commercial either explicitly states or implies all but (D). It makes no reference to how long it will take to fall asleep or how quickly the drug works. It does, however, claim to provide a restful, good night's sleep, with added energy and no aftereffects the next morning.

25. (D) Since no blue-eyed swimmer is an Olympic winner, then no blue-eyed swimmer may be a freestyle swimmer, since *all* freestyle swimmers are Olympic winners. (B) and (E) are false because they exclude other possibilities which may, in fact, exist.

26. (C) All of the other choices may be conditions that the writer fails to realize. However, only (C) is the crucial condition: since the product was purchased "several years ago," the twelve-month guarantee is no longer valid.

SECTION V: ANALYTICAL REASONING

Questions 1 to 6 are most easily solved by first making a simple chart from the information given.

	Mon.	Tues.	Wed.	Thurs.
Liz	N	N	N	AN*
Jenni	N	AN	N	N
Jolie	AN	A	N	N
Rick	A	AN	AN	AN

*afternoon and night

1. (C) Wednesday and Thursday, by referring to the chart.

2. (D) Since they could all study together on Wednesday and Thursday, Monday and Tuesday are the only possible days. Choice (A) is incorrect because they could study together more than twice on the two days.

3. (C) By referring to the chart.

4. (D) I is false, because they could all study together on Wednesday. II is true because the only afternoon Liz could study was Thursday. III is true because Jolie and Jenni could study together Monday, Tuesday, and Wednesday. Therefore, II and III are true.

5. (A) Since the four could study together on Wednesday night and Thursday night, Dan would have to be available on one of those two nights. The only choice given is Wednesday night, (A).

6. (D) On Wednesday afternoon, only Rick is available to study.

Questions 7 to 14 are more easily answered after constructing a simple diagram and filling in the places. Notice that you could answer some of the questions without the diagram. From statement 1, place Bernard across from the dentist.

Bernard

dentist

142

(Bernard is now obviously not the dentist.)
From statement 7, you could tentatively place the general practitioner and the optometrist.

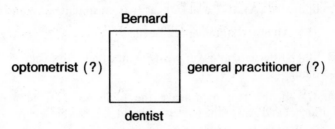

Statement 4 tells you that Carla is the general practitioner. Now you can deduce that Bernard must be the surgeon, and since Doug is not across from the surgeon (statement 2), then Doug must be the optometrist.

The final placement can be made from statement 3, because Amy must be the dentist, and the optometrist (Doug) must be on Amy's left.

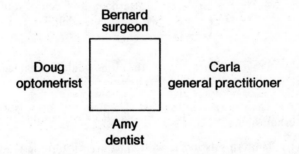

7. (C) Statement 4 says that Carla is the general practitioner, therefore you already knew that the general practitioner could not be on Carla's left (statement 6).

8. (D) I is false from statement 1. II is false from statement 5. III is true. Since statement 7 tells you that the general practitioner is across from the optometrist, the dentist must be across from the surgeon. This question could have been answered easily from the diagram.

9. (A) I must be true by looking at the diagram.

10. (C) It is evident that both I and II are true by referring to the diagram.

11. (B) Once again, this is evident from the diagram. You could have eliminated (A), (C), and (D) easily from statements 3 and 4.

12. (E) All of the statements are true.

13. (C) If Bernard and Amy switch seats, they still sit across from each other.

14. (D) If the two men leave the table, Carla (the general practitioner) and Amy (the dentist) remain at the table.

Questions 15 to 19 are not difficult to solve if an accurate map is constructed. It is important to realize that as one moves to the left, one is going west, and to the right, going east. When traveling to the west, a person will come across the eastern border first. The map should look something like this:

	Bongo	Congo	
West Water	D B E	C F A G	East Water

15. (D) Traveling east to west, the cities would be reached in this order: G, A, F, C, E.

16. (A) The sun rises in the east. The first city to see it would be the easternmost city, "G."

17. (E) The sun sets in the west. The last city to see it would be the westernmost city, "D."

18. (D) As the map shows, "B" is the capital of Bongo and "A" is the capital of Congo. City "C" is a Congo city, not a Bongo city.

19. (C) City "E" is the city on the eastern border of Bongo, the westernmost country.

From the information given, the following chart may be constructed, which would enable you to more easily answer questions 20 to 26.

	FLOOR NUMBER	PEOPLE ON	PEOPLE GET ON	PEOPLE GET OFF
STOP AT	5			
	4			
	3			
STOP AT	2		3	at least 1
	1	3		

Note that there must be at least one more stop to add to get three stops.

20. (A) For three people to get on the elevator at the second floor, at least one person must first get off because the elevator can accommodate only five people at any one time.

21. (D) Since the elevator stops at the fifth floor with five people and the total weight may not exceed 1,000 pounds, then the average weight of the people at the fifth floor must not exceed 200 pounds.

22. (B) Only statement II *must* be false. The elevator may make a stop at the third floor, and it is possible that no one gets on at the fourth floor. But someone *must* get off at the second floor to accommodate the three people getting on.

23. (E) If the elevator stops at the second floor, the third, and finally at the fifth floor, it has made its three stops and must therefore not stop at the fourth floor.

24. (A) If the elevator doesn't stop at the second floor and no one gets off at the third or fourth floors, then a total of two people must get on at floors 3 and 4 for the total to be five people by the fifth floor. Then statement I must be true.

25. (E) The elevator can only accommodate five people at any one time. If the elevator reaches the fifth floor with five people, and two people get on at that floor, *at least* two people must have gotten off at that stop.

26. (B) If the rules are still obeyed (with the exception of rule 3), then the elevator cannot go back down (see rule 4). Thus statement I is false. Rule 5 precludes a total weight of more than 1,000 pounds. Thus only statement II could possibly be true.

SECTION VI: READING COMPREHENSION

1. (C) Choices (A), (B), and (E) are all subsidiary purposes of the passage, and (D) contradicts the author's repeated mention that empirical studies do not verify therapeutic approaches. In general, the passage explains the reasons that a clinician might focus on one sound rather than another during therapy.

2. (C) We are told in the second paragraph that clinicians select early sounds for treatment based on the rationale that sounds acquired at an earlier age should be easier to teach. Thus they should be easier to learn.

3. (D) Toward the end of the third paragraph, we are told that one can more easily "see" the production of /f/.

4. (B) None of the other choices is supported in the passage, which states that the misarticulation of a rare sound is not considered a disorder.

5. (D) By comparing *steal* and *smell,* the author demonstrates that a phonetic context is defined by the relationship between adjacent sounds, for example, the relationship between *s* and *t* as compared to the relationship between *s* and *m*.

6. (E) As explained in the explanation to question 4, frequency of occurrence is emphasized in the passage as a factor in sound selection; elsewhere at several points we read that clinicians take into account the difficulty of the sound as well. Each of the other choices expressly contradicts information in the passage, except for (B), which at most is only implied by the author.

7. (E) Throughout the passage, the author mentions more than once that some rationales for sound selection have not been supported by empirical research.

8. (C) Each of the other choices is explicitly mentioned as something Skinner would support, but in the final paragraph, we read of his recognition that behaviorism is offensive to many people—that it does *not* have popular appeal.

9. (A) The sixth paragraph discusses the possible applicability of Skinner's theory to the field of human affairs, and by stressing the

relationship of behaviorism to the development of "man and society," implies its political import.

10. (B) The final paragraph mentions the popular belief that a spontaneous "will" controls human actions, and that such a belief weakens the appeal of behaviorism. The objection thus raised in this paragraph might then be juxtaposed with the evidence that behavior *can* in fact be predicted—which would then cause us consternation. Note too the grammatical appropriateness of the continuing first person plural.

11. (E) Skinner's theory is based on the belief that the "inner workings of the mind" cannot be measured accurately or conclusively; (E) would counter this belief and thus weaken the theory.

12. (A) We are told that Skinner was "obviously influenced" by Watson but that his work followed primarily from others (paragraph 3).

13. (B) Following the description of the "Skinner box" in the second paragraph (which details the stimulus-response behavior it promotes), we are told that Skinner has generalized from his success training animals in the box "laws of learning" that apply to all animals, especially humans in the more complex "box" of their academic education.

14. (E) Although paragraph 6 suggests that Skinner's theory might be applied more broadly to the control of human society, the author never indicates whether it *has*. Each of the other choices is a question answered in the passage.

15. (C) This situation establishes a relationship between price and quantity which parallels the paragraph 2 explanation of the "law of demand." This section discusses "the consumer's desire to get the 'best buy,' " and goes on to say that "if the price of good A increases, the individual will tend to substitute another good and purchase less of good A." Since the appearance of a lower-priced breakfast drink makes orange juice more "expensive," in relation, the law of demand as so described would prevail.

16. (D) The third paragraph distinguishes "individual demand" and "market demand"; the former is exercised by a single person, whereas the latter is exerted by a *group* of individuals. With this

distinction in mind, we may conclude that a group of individuals constitutes a market. (B) contradicts the paragraph. (A), (C), and (E) might be true under certain conditions, but those conditions are not specified in the question or in the passage.

17. (A) Initially, the passage emphasizes a distinction between "demand" and "quantity demanded," concluding that "demand shifts when there is a change in income, expectations, taste, etc., such that a different quantity of the good is demanded at the *same* price." This statement fits (A) precisely. All other choices include or allow for a *changing* price.

18. (B) Paragraph 4 states, "there is a positive correlation between quantity supplied and product price." Since that means that quantity and price are related, any choice (in this case all choices except B) with a relational connotation does not tell us what the two items are *not*.

19. (C) The passage says that "demand shifts when there is a change in income, expectations, taste, etc., such that a different quantity of the good is demanded at the same price." (A), (D), and (E) all involve a *changing* price, and (B) would reduce income so that demand would *decrease*.

20. (B) The last sentence says that it is "developed" or "interdependent" economies that acquiesce to the idea that government must control economy to some extent. This leaves underdeveloped countries unspoken for and raises the possibility they might *not* acquiesce to government control.

21. (B) The paragraph states that government action "may create shortages or surpluses." Shortages and surpluses are associated with disequilibrium in paragraph 6.

22. (B) The author uses *qua* in the midst of stressing the human tendency to *compare* the characteristics of inanimate objects to human characteristics.

23. (C) Each of the paragraphs is enclosed in quotation marks, and the phrase "to quote his own words" in the first paragraph clearly indicates that the author is recording a viewpoint other than his or her own.

24. (A) The bulk of the speaker's argument creates the case that presumably unconscious entities—the vapour engine, the potato, the oyster—do possess a sort of consciousness if looked at from an unconventional point of view.

25. (D) The main argument of the passage, that presumably unconscious things do possess a sort of consciousness, is summarized in the first sentence of the fourth paragraph; the opposite case (no consciousness) is also summarized here, but the summary of the main argument is nevertheless present.

26. (E) In this paragraph the speaker implies this belief with the rhetorical question, "Is not everything interwoven with everything?"

27. (B) When discussing potatoes and oysters in the third paragraph, the speaker points out that we suppose that such creatures do not have emotions because they make no sounds, thus implying that they may indeed have emotions, which are invisible to our limited, conventional human perception.

28. (C) In the third paragraph, the author stresses the human tendency to understand other creatures *qua* mankind and implies the limitations of such understanding with several phrases, notably "but mankind is not everybody."

PRACTICE TEST 2

ANSWER SHEET FOR PRACTICE TEST 2
(Remove This Sheet and Use It to Mark Your Answers)

CUT HERE

SECTION I	SECTION II	SECTION III

SECTION I

1 Ⓐ Ⓑ Ⓒ Ⓓ Ⓔ
2 Ⓐ Ⓑ Ⓒ Ⓓ Ⓔ
3 Ⓐ Ⓑ Ⓒ Ⓓ Ⓔ
4 Ⓐ Ⓑ Ⓒ Ⓓ Ⓔ
5 Ⓐ Ⓑ Ⓒ Ⓓ Ⓔ
6 Ⓐ Ⓑ Ⓒ Ⓓ Ⓔ
7 Ⓐ Ⓑ Ⓒ Ⓓ Ⓔ
8 Ⓐ Ⓑ Ⓒ Ⓓ Ⓔ
9 Ⓐ Ⓑ Ⓒ Ⓓ Ⓔ
10 Ⓐ Ⓑ Ⓒ Ⓓ Ⓔ
11 Ⓐ Ⓑ Ⓒ Ⓓ Ⓔ
12 Ⓐ Ⓑ Ⓒ Ⓓ Ⓔ
13 Ⓐ Ⓑ Ⓒ Ⓓ Ⓔ
14 Ⓐ Ⓑ Ⓒ Ⓓ Ⓔ
15 Ⓐ Ⓑ Ⓒ Ⓓ Ⓔ
16 Ⓐ Ⓑ Ⓒ Ⓓ Ⓔ
17 Ⓐ Ⓑ Ⓒ Ⓓ Ⓔ
18 Ⓐ Ⓑ Ⓒ Ⓓ Ⓔ
19 Ⓐ Ⓑ Ⓒ Ⓓ Ⓔ
20 Ⓐ Ⓑ Ⓒ Ⓓ Ⓔ
21 Ⓐ Ⓑ Ⓒ Ⓓ Ⓔ
22 Ⓐ Ⓑ Ⓒ Ⓓ Ⓔ
23 Ⓐ Ⓑ Ⓒ Ⓓ Ⓔ
24 Ⓐ Ⓑ Ⓒ Ⓓ Ⓔ
25 Ⓐ Ⓑ Ⓒ Ⓓ Ⓔ
26 Ⓐ Ⓑ Ⓒ Ⓓ Ⓔ

SECTION II

1 Ⓐ Ⓑ Ⓒ Ⓓ Ⓔ
2 Ⓐ Ⓑ Ⓒ Ⓓ Ⓔ
3 Ⓐ Ⓑ Ⓒ Ⓓ Ⓔ
4 Ⓐ Ⓑ Ⓒ Ⓓ Ⓔ
5 Ⓐ Ⓑ Ⓒ Ⓓ Ⓔ
6 Ⓐ Ⓑ Ⓒ Ⓓ Ⓔ
7 Ⓐ Ⓑ Ⓒ Ⓓ Ⓔ
8 Ⓐ Ⓑ Ⓒ Ⓓ Ⓔ
9 Ⓐ Ⓑ Ⓒ Ⓓ Ⓔ
10 Ⓐ Ⓑ Ⓒ Ⓓ Ⓔ
11 Ⓐ Ⓑ Ⓒ Ⓓ Ⓔ
12 Ⓐ Ⓑ Ⓒ Ⓓ Ⓔ
13 Ⓐ Ⓑ Ⓒ Ⓓ Ⓔ
14 Ⓐ Ⓑ Ⓒ Ⓓ Ⓔ
15 Ⓐ Ⓑ Ⓒ Ⓓ Ⓔ
16 Ⓐ Ⓑ Ⓒ Ⓓ Ⓔ
17 Ⓐ Ⓑ Ⓒ Ⓓ Ⓔ
18 Ⓐ Ⓑ Ⓒ Ⓓ Ⓔ
19 Ⓐ Ⓑ Ⓒ Ⓓ Ⓔ
20 Ⓐ Ⓑ Ⓒ Ⓓ Ⓔ
21 Ⓐ Ⓑ Ⓒ Ⓓ Ⓔ
22 Ⓐ Ⓑ Ⓒ Ⓓ Ⓔ
23 Ⓐ Ⓑ Ⓒ Ⓓ Ⓔ
24 Ⓐ Ⓑ Ⓒ Ⓓ Ⓔ
25 Ⓐ Ⓑ Ⓒ Ⓓ Ⓔ
26 Ⓐ Ⓑ Ⓒ Ⓓ Ⓔ
27 Ⓐ Ⓑ Ⓒ Ⓓ Ⓔ
28 Ⓐ Ⓑ Ⓒ Ⓓ Ⓔ
29 Ⓐ Ⓑ Ⓒ Ⓓ Ⓔ
30 Ⓐ Ⓑ Ⓒ Ⓓ Ⓔ

31 Ⓐ Ⓑ Ⓒ Ⓓ Ⓔ
32 Ⓐ Ⓑ Ⓒ Ⓓ Ⓔ
33 Ⓐ Ⓑ Ⓒ Ⓓ Ⓔ
34 Ⓐ Ⓑ Ⓒ Ⓓ Ⓔ
35 Ⓐ Ⓑ Ⓒ Ⓓ Ⓔ
36 Ⓐ Ⓑ Ⓒ Ⓓ Ⓔ
37 Ⓐ Ⓑ Ⓒ Ⓓ Ⓔ
38 Ⓐ Ⓑ Ⓒ Ⓓ Ⓔ
39 Ⓐ Ⓑ Ⓒ Ⓓ Ⓔ

SECTION III

1 Ⓐ Ⓑ Ⓒ Ⓓ Ⓔ
2 Ⓐ Ⓑ Ⓒ Ⓓ Ⓔ
3 Ⓐ Ⓑ Ⓒ Ⓓ Ⓔ
4 Ⓐ Ⓑ Ⓒ Ⓓ Ⓔ
5 Ⓐ Ⓑ Ⓒ Ⓓ Ⓔ
6 Ⓐ Ⓑ Ⓒ Ⓓ Ⓔ
7 Ⓐ Ⓑ Ⓒ Ⓓ Ⓔ
8 Ⓐ Ⓑ Ⓒ Ⓓ Ⓔ
9 Ⓐ Ⓑ Ⓒ Ⓓ Ⓔ
10 Ⓐ Ⓑ Ⓒ Ⓓ Ⓔ
11 Ⓐ Ⓑ Ⓒ Ⓓ Ⓔ
12 Ⓐ Ⓑ Ⓒ Ⓓ Ⓔ
13 Ⓐ Ⓑ Ⓒ Ⓓ Ⓔ
14 Ⓐ Ⓑ Ⓒ Ⓓ Ⓔ
15 Ⓐ Ⓑ Ⓒ Ⓓ Ⓔ
16 Ⓐ Ⓑ Ⓒ Ⓓ Ⓔ
17 Ⓐ Ⓑ Ⓒ Ⓓ Ⓔ
18 Ⓐ Ⓑ Ⓒ Ⓓ Ⓔ
19 Ⓐ Ⓑ Ⓒ Ⓓ Ⓔ
20 Ⓐ Ⓑ Ⓒ Ⓓ Ⓔ
21 Ⓐ Ⓑ Ⓒ Ⓓ Ⓔ
22 Ⓐ Ⓑ Ⓒ Ⓓ Ⓔ
23 Ⓐ Ⓑ Ⓒ Ⓓ Ⓔ
24 Ⓐ Ⓑ Ⓒ Ⓓ Ⓔ
25 Ⓐ Ⓑ Ⓒ Ⓓ Ⓔ
26 Ⓐ Ⓑ Ⓒ Ⓓ Ⓔ
27 Ⓐ Ⓑ Ⓒ Ⓓ Ⓔ

ANSWER SHEET FOR PRACTICE TEST 2
(Remove This Sheet and Use It to Mark Your Answers)

SECTION IV

1 Ⓐ Ⓑ Ⓒ Ⓓ Ⓔ
2 Ⓐ Ⓑ Ⓒ Ⓓ Ⓔ
3 Ⓐ Ⓑ Ⓒ Ⓓ Ⓔ
4 Ⓐ Ⓑ Ⓒ Ⓓ Ⓔ
5 Ⓐ Ⓑ Ⓒ Ⓓ Ⓔ
6 Ⓐ Ⓑ Ⓒ Ⓓ Ⓔ
7 Ⓐ Ⓑ Ⓒ Ⓓ Ⓔ
8 Ⓐ Ⓑ Ⓒ Ⓓ Ⓔ
9 Ⓐ Ⓑ Ⓒ Ⓓ Ⓔ
10 Ⓐ Ⓑ Ⓒ Ⓓ Ⓔ
11 Ⓐ Ⓑ Ⓒ Ⓓ Ⓔ
12 Ⓐ Ⓑ Ⓒ Ⓓ Ⓔ
13 Ⓐ Ⓑ Ⓒ Ⓓ Ⓔ
14 Ⓐ Ⓑ Ⓒ Ⓓ Ⓔ
15 Ⓐ Ⓑ Ⓒ Ⓓ Ⓔ
16 Ⓐ Ⓑ Ⓒ Ⓓ Ⓔ
17 Ⓐ Ⓑ Ⓒ Ⓓ Ⓔ
18 Ⓐ Ⓑ Ⓒ Ⓓ Ⓔ
19 Ⓐ Ⓑ Ⓒ Ⓓ Ⓔ
20 Ⓐ Ⓑ Ⓒ Ⓓ Ⓔ
21 Ⓐ Ⓑ Ⓒ Ⓓ Ⓔ
22 Ⓐ Ⓑ Ⓒ Ⓓ Ⓔ
23 Ⓐ Ⓑ Ⓒ Ⓓ Ⓔ
24 Ⓐ Ⓑ Ⓒ Ⓓ Ⓔ
25 Ⓐ Ⓑ Ⓒ Ⓓ Ⓔ
26 Ⓐ Ⓑ Ⓒ Ⓓ Ⓔ
27 Ⓐ Ⓑ Ⓒ Ⓓ Ⓔ

SECTION V

1 Ⓐ Ⓑ Ⓒ Ⓓ Ⓔ
2 Ⓐ Ⓑ Ⓒ Ⓓ Ⓔ
3 Ⓐ Ⓑ Ⓒ Ⓓ Ⓔ
4 Ⓐ Ⓑ Ⓒ Ⓓ Ⓔ
5 Ⓐ Ⓑ Ⓒ Ⓓ Ⓔ
6 Ⓐ Ⓑ Ⓒ Ⓓ Ⓔ
7 Ⓐ Ⓑ Ⓒ Ⓓ Ⓔ
8 Ⓐ Ⓑ Ⓒ Ⓓ Ⓔ
9 Ⓐ Ⓑ Ⓒ Ⓓ Ⓔ
10 Ⓐ Ⓑ Ⓒ Ⓓ Ⓔ
11 Ⓐ Ⓑ Ⓒ Ⓓ Ⓔ
12 Ⓐ Ⓑ Ⓒ Ⓓ Ⓔ
13 Ⓐ Ⓑ Ⓒ Ⓓ Ⓔ
14 Ⓐ Ⓑ Ⓒ Ⓓ Ⓔ
15 Ⓐ Ⓑ Ⓒ Ⓓ Ⓔ
16 Ⓐ Ⓑ Ⓒ Ⓓ Ⓔ
17 Ⓐ Ⓑ Ⓒ Ⓓ Ⓔ
18 Ⓐ Ⓑ Ⓒ Ⓓ Ⓔ
19 Ⓐ Ⓑ Ⓒ Ⓓ Ⓔ
20 Ⓐ Ⓑ Ⓒ Ⓓ Ⓔ
21 Ⓐ Ⓑ Ⓒ Ⓓ Ⓔ
22 Ⓐ Ⓑ Ⓒ Ⓓ Ⓔ
23 Ⓐ Ⓑ Ⓒ Ⓓ Ⓔ
24 Ⓐ Ⓑ Ⓒ Ⓓ Ⓔ
25 Ⓐ Ⓑ Ⓒ Ⓓ Ⓔ
26 Ⓐ Ⓑ Ⓒ Ⓓ Ⓔ

SECTION VI

1 Ⓐ Ⓑ Ⓒ Ⓓ Ⓔ
2 Ⓐ Ⓑ Ⓒ Ⓓ Ⓔ
3 Ⓐ Ⓑ Ⓒ Ⓓ Ⓔ
4 Ⓐ Ⓑ Ⓒ Ⓓ Ⓔ
5 Ⓐ Ⓑ Ⓒ Ⓓ Ⓔ
6 Ⓐ Ⓑ Ⓒ Ⓓ Ⓔ
7 Ⓐ Ⓑ Ⓒ Ⓓ Ⓔ
8 Ⓐ Ⓑ Ⓒ Ⓓ Ⓔ
9 Ⓐ Ⓑ Ⓒ Ⓓ Ⓔ
10 Ⓐ Ⓑ Ⓒ Ⓓ Ⓔ
11 Ⓐ Ⓑ Ⓒ Ⓓ Ⓔ
12 Ⓐ Ⓑ Ⓒ Ⓓ Ⓔ
13 Ⓐ Ⓑ Ⓒ Ⓓ Ⓔ
14 Ⓐ Ⓑ Ⓒ Ⓓ Ⓔ
15 Ⓐ Ⓑ Ⓒ Ⓓ Ⓔ
16 Ⓐ Ⓑ Ⓒ Ⓓ Ⓔ
17 Ⓐ Ⓑ Ⓒ Ⓓ Ⓔ
18 Ⓐ Ⓑ Ⓒ Ⓓ Ⓔ
19 Ⓐ Ⓑ Ⓒ Ⓓ Ⓔ
20 Ⓐ Ⓑ Ⓒ Ⓓ Ⓔ
21 Ⓐ Ⓑ Ⓒ Ⓓ Ⓔ
22 Ⓐ Ⓑ Ⓒ Ⓓ Ⓔ
23 Ⓐ Ⓑ Ⓒ Ⓓ Ⓔ
24 Ⓐ Ⓑ Ⓒ Ⓓ Ⓔ
25 Ⓐ Ⓑ Ⓒ Ⓓ Ⓔ
26 Ⓐ Ⓑ Ⓒ Ⓓ Ⓔ

- - CUT HERE - -

WRITING ESSAY

Time: 30 Minutes

DIRECTIONS

You are to complete a brief essay on the given topic. You may take no more than 30 minutes to plan and write your essay. After reading the topic carefully, you should probably spend a few minutes planning and organizing your response. YOU MAY NOT WRITE ON A TOPIC OTHER THAN THE GIVEN TOPIC.

The quality of your writing is more important than either the quantity of writing or the point of view you adopt. Your skill in organization, mechanics, and usage is important, although it is expected that your essay will not be flawless because of the time pressure under which you write.

Keep your writing within the lined area of your essay booklet. Write on every line, avoid wide margins, and write carefully and legibly.

Essay Topic

Read the following description of Sendak and Krull, candidates for promotion to staff supervisor at the software manufacturing firm of Bytonics, Inc. *Then, in the space provided, write an argument for promoting either Sendak or Krull.* Use the information in this description and assume that two general policies guide the promotion decisions at Bytonics:

1. Promotions are based on a combination of experience and effectiveness on the job.
2. Effectiveness on the job is measured by periodic on-site evaluations, evidence of innovative ideas, and reliable completion of assigned tasks.

Sendak earned a master's degree in computer science before joining Bytonics, where she has worked for five years. She was a computer enthusiast long before it was fashionable, designing new software for local businesses while she was still in high school. At Bytonics, she has received an on-site evaluation twice each year, and all but one of the several managers who have observed her

155

work filed positive reports. As the competition among software firms has continued to increase, Sendak has been partly responsible for the strong position of Bytonics. Working overtime often, she has developed a series of new programs for teaching foreign languages to elementary school students. The programs have been adopted and used effectively by a number of schools throughout the country. As well as having created these programs, Sendak has managed to carry out all of her assigned tasks fully and efficiently.

Krull has worked at Bytonics for fifteen years, since her graduation from high school. She began as a messenger and quickly learned the essentials of computer software by persistently asking intelligent questions of the company experts and volunteering for progressively more challenging software tasks. Her thirty on-site evaluations all contain lavish praise; managers note especially her reliability. Any task she is given, no matter how difficult, will be seen to successful completion. Although Krull has not designed any original software as yet, she is a talented critic of others' ideas and has offered perceptive advice that has helped improve a number of new Bytonics products.

SECTION I: LOGICAL REASONING

Time: 35 Minutes
26 Questions

DIRECTIONS

You will be presented with brief passages or statements and will be required to evaluate their reasoning. In each case, select the best answer choice, even though more than one choice may present a possible answer. Choices which are unreasonable or incompatible with common-sense standards should be eliminated.

Aristotle said that art represents "general truths" about human nature. Our city councilman is arguing in favor of the artistry—a giant mural in front of a Jeep dealership, portraying a variety of four-wheel-drive vehicles. He cites Aristotle's conception of art as his support.

1. The passage above raises which of the following questions?
   (A) Can a city councilman understand Aristotle?
   (B) Which general truths about human nature does a four-wheel-drive mural *not* represent?
   (C) Could Aristotle have predicted a modern society filled with sophisticated machines?
   (D) To what extent are four-wheel-drive vehicles representative of a general advance in modern technology?
   (E) What "general truth" about human nature does a mural of four-wheel-drive vehicles represent?

2. *Speaker 1:* The holy passion of friendship is of so sweet and steady and loyal and enduring a nature that it will last through a whole lifetime.
   Speaker 2: If not asked to lend money.

   The two speakers represent which of the following contrasting attitudes?
   (A) faith and despair
   (B) idealism and cynicism
   (C) idealism and optimism
   (D) socialism and capitalism
   (E) friendship and enmity

157

In 1933, a new industrial code was established to fix a minimum wage of 40 cents an hour in the United States.

3. The above statement suggests which of the following maxims, or proverbs?
   (A) You can fool some of the people some of the time.
   (B) Don't count your chickens before they hatch.
   (C) Times change.
   (D) There's a sucker born every minute.
   (E) Power to the people.

Unfortunately, only 11 percent of the driving public uses regular seat belts. Automatic restraints are the answer, and the quicker they are required, the sooner highways deaths will be reduced.

4. The author's conclusion is based upon which of the following assumptions?
   (A) Only 11 percent of the driving public cares about passengers' lives.
   (B) The use of restraints reduces highway deaths.
   (C) Regular seat belts are inadequate safety devices.
   (D) It is unfortunate that 89 percent of the driving public does not use regular seat belts.
   (E) Highway deaths occur often enough so that reducing them is a necessity.

Questions 5 and 6 refer to the following passage

The heart and soul of our business is credibility. We get that credibility and respect, and the power that goes with it, only by being a socially and professionally responsible agent for the public. In some ways we journalists have to have the same attitude to news as an employee of a bank has to money—it isn't ours. We're handling it on behalf of other people, so it cannot be converted to our own use. If we do, it's embezzlement.

5. Which of the following criticisms would most weaken the comparison between journalists and bank employees?
   (A) Different newspapers print different news, just as different banks hold assets from various sources.
   (B) Journalists are necessarily more creative individuals than bank employees.
   (C) The heart and soul of the banking business is money, not credibility.
   (D) A bank teller need not be credible, just responsible.
   (E) Embezzlement is properly a crime against the bank, not against the depositors.

6. The first sentence makes a point with which of the following techniques?
   (A) metaphor   (D) overstatement
   (B) sarcasm   (E) statistical support
   (C) parody

The value of a close examination of the circumstances of an aircraft accident lies not only in fixing blame but in learning lessons.

7. The above statement fits most logically into which of the following types of passages?
   (A) a survey of the "scapegoat phenomenon" in modern society
   (B) an argument in favor of including specific details in any academic essay
   (C) an argument against the usefulness of the National Transportation Safety Board
   (D) a brief history of aeronautics
   (E) a description of the causes of a particular aircraft accident

Consumers are not so easily manipulated as they are often painted. They may know what they want, and what they want may be greatly different from what other people believe they need.

8. Which of the following statements, if true, most weakens the above argument?
   (A) Most people continue to buy the same brand of a product year after year.
   (B) Companies that advertise the most sell the most products.
   (C) Store shelves packed with a variety of different brands have the potential to confuse the consumer.
   (D) Most consumers know which brand they are going to buy before entering a store.
   (E) People who shop with others rarely argue with their companions.

Questions 9 and 10 refer to the following passage

The last census showed a sharp rise during the 1970s in the number of Americans living together as unmarried couples, but a more recent increase in the marriage rate in 1981 suggests that matrimony will make a comeback in the 1980s.

9. Which of the following best refutes the argument above?
   (A) One of the causes of more marriages is that the large population resulting from a baby boom is just now reaching marriageable age.
   (B) Although information about the 1981 marriage rate is not complete, most analysts consider it to be reliable.
   (C) Many of those marrying in 1981 were couples who had lived together during the 1970s.
   (D) The number of Americans living together did not rise at a consistent rate during the 1970s.
   (E) The marriage rate increased dramatically in 1971 and fell even more dramatically in following years.

10. With which of the following would the author be likely to agree?
    (A) Americans should not live together as unmarried couples.
    (B) Matrimony is preferable to living together.
    (C) Economic circumstances have made matrimony attractive as a way of paying less income tax.
    (D) The attitudes of young people in the 1980s are altogether different from the attitudes of young people in the 1970s.
    (E) Prevailing attitudes toward marriage tend to persist for more than one year.

The shortsightedness of our government and our scientists has virtually nullified all of their great discoveries because of their failure to consider the environmental impact. The situation is far from hopeless, but our government agencies must become better watchdogs.

11. This argument fails to place any blame on
    I. consumers who prefer new technology to clean air
    II. the ability of government to actually police industry
    III. legal loopholes which allow industry abuse of government regulations

    (A) I only   (D) I, II, and III
    (B) II only   (E) I and III
    (C) III only

Voltaire once said, "Common sense is not so common."

12. Which of the following most nearly parallels Voltaire's statement?
    (A) God must have loved the common man; he certainly made enough of them.
    (B) The common good is not necessarily best for everyone.
    (C) Jumbo shrimp may not actually be very big.
    (D) Good people may not necessarily have good sense.
    (E) Truth serum cannot contain the truth.

Questions 13 and 14 refer to the following passage

The department store owned by my competitor sells green necklaces that glow in the dark. Only those customers of mine wearing those necklaces must be giving business to the competition.

13. The conclusion could best be strengthened by
    (A) deleting *that glow in the dark*
    (B) changing *sells* to *has sold*
    (C) changing *the competition* to *my competitor*
    (D) inserting *only* as the first word in sentence one
    (E) changing *wearing* to *owning*

14. The author foolishly assumes that
    (A) the customers might find the necklaces attractive
    (B) customers are not buying other products from the competi-
        tion
    (C) customers will wear the necklaces in daylight
    (D) a department store should not sell necklaces
    (E) the competition is outselling the author

15. Which of the following most logically completes the passage at
    the blank below?

    Several of the survivors discussed their dilemma. They could
    remain on the island and attempt to survive as best they knew
    how. Or they could attempt to escape, using the resources
    available to them. None of the group wished to venture away
    from their uncertain sanctuary, but all of them knew that help
    would be a long time coming. Their discussions were thus
    _____.

    (A) futile, arbitrary, and capricious
    (B) limited by their imagination and resolve
    (C) dampened by a sense of impending doom
    (D) possible, but by no means successful
    (E) courageous and honorable

Questions 16 and 17 refer to the following letter

To the Chairman:

    At the October 7th meeting it was decided that no two officers
would hold positions on the same committee. It has recently
come to my attention that both Charles S. Smith and Arnold
Krunkle will be serving in some capacity on the Building and
Maintenance Committee, and both have been nominated for
officer status. As you know, this is in direct disregard for the
rules as voted by the membership last October 7th. I would hope
that sufficient action be taken by the Disciplinary Committee

(on which committee both of the above are members) so that this problem will be remedied.

Sincerely,

Irving H. Fortnash

16. Which of the following is the essential flaw that the writer of the letter fails to notice?
    (A) Smith and Krunkle are already serving together on the Disciplinary Committee.
    (B) The Chairman has no power in the matter.
    (C) The membership cannot pass rules limiting members.
    (D) Smith and Krunkle are not yet officers.
    (E) Building and Maintenance is actually two committees.

17. Which of the following most completely and reasonably describes actions that may occur in the near future?
    (A) Fortnash resigns his membership.
    (B) Either Smith or Krunkle resigns his membership.
    (C) Krunkle resigns his committee post on the Building and Maintenance Committee.
    (D) Smith resigns his position on the Building and Maintenance Committee.
    (E) One of the two (Smith or Krunkle) resigns his position on the Building and Maintenance Committee, and the other resigns his position on the Disciplinary Committee.

Flamo Lighters when you need them! Always reliable, always dependable. In all weather, with ten-year guarantee. Don't get caught without a light—keep a Flamo in your pocket wherever you go!

18. All of the following are claims made or implied by Flamo Lighters *except*
    (A) convenience   (D) winter-proof
    (B) dependability   (E) all-purpose
    (C) longevity

Questions 19 through 21 refer to the following statements

(A) The skating team of Roscoe and Nordoff is obviously the best. They are more graceful and more pleasing to the eye than any of the other skaters.

(B) Newspaper reporters have a commitment to report only the truth. Since only the truth may be printed, reporters must seek it out.

(C) And who can argue that winning the war against poverty isn't foremost? It is the terrible affliction of our time.

(D) All records of births, deaths, and marriages are doubtful, since all these records are open to question.

(E) The quality of American goods far surpasses any of the imports; after all, we pay far less money for Japanese televisions.

19. Which statement supports its conclusion by using a subjective basis of comparison?

20. Which statement uses a probable irrelevancy to support its point?

21. Which statement supports itself by redundancy?

All race-car lovers enjoy classical music.
No backgammon players enjoy classical music.
All those who enjoy classical music also enjoy fine wine.

22. If each of the above statements is true, which of the following must also be true?
    (A) Everyone who plays backgammon enjoys fine wine.
    (B) No one who enjoys fine wine plays backgammon.
    (C) No backgammon players are race-car lovers.
    (D) No backgammon players enjoy fine wine.
    (E) No race-car lover enjoys fine wine.

Questions 23 through 25 refer to the following passage

It has been proven that the "lie detector" can be fooled. If one is truly unaware that one is lying, when in fact one is, then the "lie detector" is worthless.

23. The author of this argument implies that
    (A) the lie detector is a useless device
    (B) a good liar can fool the device
    (C) a lie detector is often inaccurate
    (D) the lie detector is sometimes worthless
    (E) no one can fool the lie detector all of the time

24. This argument would be strengthened most by
    (A) demonstrating that one's awareness of truth or falsity is always undetectable
    (B) showing that the "truth" of any statement always relies on a subjective assessment
    (C) citing evidence that there are other means of measuring truth which are consistently less reliable than the lie detector
    (D) citing the number of cases in which the lie detector mistook falsehood for truth
    (E) claiming that ordinary, unbiased people are the best "lie detectors"

25. Without contradicting his or her own statements, the author might present which of the following arguments as a strong point in favor of the lie detector?
    (A) The methodology used by investigative critics of lie detectors is itself highly flawed.
    (B) Law-enforcement agencies have purchased too many detectors to abandon them now.
    (C) Circumstantial evidence might be more useful in a criminal case than is personal testimony.
    (D) The very threat of a lie-detector test has led a significant number of criminals to confess.
    (E) People are never "truly unaware" that they are lying.

The water quality of Lake Tahoe—the largest, deepest, high mountain lake in North America—is steadily diminishing. Protecting its delicate ecological balance is essential.

26. Which of the following arguments most closely resembles the argument above?
    (A) The ability of many famous artists of the 1930s is steadily diminishing. Encouraging their continued productivity is essential.
    (B) Erosion has taken its toll on Mt. Rushmore, defacing the historical monument. Appropriating money for its repair and restoration must be given priority.
    (C) The quality of life in our older cities has ceased to be a concern to many legislators.
    (D) The water quality of Lake Erie has been a diminishing concern of both Americans and Canadians over the past decade.
    (E) The Grand Canyon, a deep natural excavation and a national monument, has steadily diminished in its appeal to tourists. Protecting its waning popularity is essential.

STOP. IF YOU FINISH BEFORE TIME IS CALLED, CHECK YOUR WORK ON THIS SECTION ONLY. DO NOT WORK ON ANY OTHER SECTION IN THE TEST.

SECTION II: DISPUTE CHARACTERIZATION

Time: 35 Minutes
39 Questions

DIRECTIONS

You are presented with a narrative of facts, a dispute, and two rules. Sometimes the rules are conflicting, sometimes not; but in any case each rule should be considered independent of the other. Questions follow each set of rules. You are to classify each question according to the following choices:

- (A) A relevant question whose answer requires a choice between the rules.
- (B) A relevant question whose answer does not require a choice between the rules but requires additional facts or rules.
- (C) A relevant question that is readily answerable from the facts or rules or both.
- (D) An irrelevant question or one whose answer bears only remotely on the outcome of the dispute.

Set 1

Facts: Zake Porton, a well-known host of a television exercise program, agreed to endorse a new frozen dessert. He was assured that the dessert contained only natural ingredients, and so he promised to advertise the product during his exercise program. However, he asked that one of his own staff be allowed to make a nutritional analysis of the product and announce the results of the analysis on the program. The staff analyst concluded that the dessert contained 60% refined sugar and 40% fruit flavorings and announced these results on the air. Porton went ahead and advertised the product on his program for several days, emphasizing that only natural ingredients were used, until he received a barrage of mail from viewers who insisted that refined sugar was not a natural ingredient. They threatened to discontinue viewing the program if his endorsements continued. Porton then appeared on his program and retracted the endorsement, claiming that he had not been aware of the results of the nutritional analysis.

Dispute: A consumers group sued Porton for false advertising. Porton contested.

Rule I: False advertising consists of promoting a product using statements which are not true.

Rule II: Only intentional misrepresentation constitutes false advertising, and only if the person making the misrepresentation stands to profit from the falsehoods.

Questions:

1. Did Porton have a large following watching the endorsements?
2. If Porton did not know that ingredients which were not natural were used, who will win the suit?
3. Did Porton stand to profit from the falsehoods?
4. If refined sugar is not a natural food and Porton stood to make a profit from the falsehoods, and if his misrepresentations were intentional, will he be found guilty of false advertising?
5. If refined sugar is not considered a natural ingredient, were Porton's statements true?
6. If Porton's statements were intentionally misleading because he knew refined sugar was not a natural food but he would not profit from them, will he be found guilty of false advertising?
7. Is refined sugar a natural ingredient?

Set 2

Facts: In order to reduce inner-city pollution, the Beerbelly Brewing Company moved its main brewery out to a relatively isolated area on the coast; there the smoke emissions caused by production were neutralized by the ocean breeze. For the drivers of the brewery delivery trucks, the new location presented difficulties; the only access road was a winding, narrow mountain trail, with barely enough space to accommodate a single truck. The company had promised to improve the road but as yet had not begun to do so. Early one afternoon, Fred Delgado, driving away from the brewery with a full load of bottled beer, encountered Mitch Dungaree, driving an empty truck in the opposite direction. Delgado swerved onto a narrow cliff to avoid the collision and was able to jump free of the truck and escape unharmed just before the truck rolled down the hill, exploded, and burned.

Dispute: Beerbelly Brewing Company sued Fred for the damages to the truck and its contents. Fred contested.

Rule I: The property owner is liable for any damages caused by inadequate entrance to the owner's property.

Rule II: A driver is responsible for the safety and maintenance of his or her truck.

Questions:

8. If the property was not owned by the Beerbelly Brewing Company, will Fred win the suit?
9. Did the company recognize the potential problem?
10. If the Brewing Company owned the property and the entrance was inadequate, who will win the suit?
11. Who caused the accident, Fred or Mitch?
12. Was the entrance to the property adequate?
13. If the entrance to the property was adequate, who owned the property?
14. If the entrance was adequate and the Beerbelly Brewing Company owned the property, who will win the suit?

Set 3

Facts: Leslie Chan was offered a very appealing position at Standard University, on the condition that she complete her doctoral dissertation within six months. Leslie decided she could finish the dissertation and take the position if she used a word processor to help her work more efficiently. She purchased a Home Mental Bank (HMB) processor from the Ready Electronics store, mainly because the store manager assured her that the HMB featured a reliable memory that could not lose information. In addition, the HMB, he said, had the largest storage capacity of all the models available. After typing three chapters of her dissertation into the word processor, Leslie decided to begin revising Chapter 1. When she commanded the processor to display page 1 of Chapter 1, the screen remained blank. After failing at repeated attempts to find various sections of her dissertation, Leslie called for a Ready Electronics serviceman, who concluded that the dissertation was not retrievable.

Dispute: Leslie sued Ready Electronics for misrepresentation to be repaid for the cost of the HMB. Ready Electronics contested.

Rule I: One is liable for misrepresentation if one intentionally falsely represents a material fact or an item.

Rule II: Items valued at over $400 can be misrepresented only if the representation is in writing.

Questions:

15. If the store manager intentionally misrepresented the HMB only verbally and the HMB cost $800, will Leslie win?
16. What was the value of the HMB?
17. If the HMB was valued at $300 and the store manager's misrepresentation was intentional, who will win?
18. Did Leslie get the position at Standard University?
19. If the store manager did not intentionally misrepresent, will Leslie win?
20. Was there a written representation regarding the HMB?

Set 4

Facts: As a member of the Discount Club, Jean was entitled to purchase automobile tires at lower than retail prices. Taking advantage of a limited offer by the Club, she purchased four tires and was assured by the Club that the tires would last for at least 25,000 miles under normal driving conditions. Jean drove a compact car which was designed so that the rear tires tilted slightly inward at the top, wearing down the inner portion of the tires more quickly than the outer portion. After 15,000 miles with her new tires, Jean noticed that the tread was worn smooth on the inner portion of each of the rear tires and knew that this much tread wear could reduce the braking ability of the car. She returned the car to the Discount Club, who declined to replace the worn tires with new ones.

Dispute: Jean sued the Discount Club for the cost of the tires. The Club contested.

Rule I: Only those written contracts or guarantees for over $100 are binding on all parties involved.

Rule II: When special conditions are involved, an addendum covering those special conditions must be written into the original contract; otherwise, there is no liability on the part of the seller.

Questions:

21. If the tires cost $250 and if there were no special conditions involved, will Jean win the suit?
22. Did Jean get a good deal on the tires?
23. If the tires cost $300 and if the guarantee and addendum covering the special conditions of her car were in writing, will Jean recover her money?
24. Was the contract in writing?
25. How much did the tires cost?
26. If the tires cost a total of $90 and the guarantee and addendum covering the special conditions of her car were in writing, will the Club win the suit?

Set 5

Facts: Dexter, a college student, decided to lease one room of Stan's large house. At the time of the final agreement, Stan also agreed to install a new roof within one month. A few months later Stan had not made even the slightest effort to do so. During a heavy snowstorm, the roof collapsed, and though Stan was unharmed, Dexter suffered serious injuries which incapacitated him for the remainder of the school semester, causing him to forfeit his tuition fees.

Dispute: Dexter sued Stan for damages. Stan contested.

Rule I: A landlord has no liability regarding the domicile leased.

Rule II: Any agreement between a landlord and tenant is binding only if the agreement is in writing, and only then is each party liable for any responsibility assumed.

Questions:

27. If the agreement between Stan and Dexter was in writing, will Dexter win the suit?
28. If the agreement was spoken, did Stan assume any liability?
29. Was the agreement between Stan and Dexter in writing?
30. If the agreement between Stan and Dexter was only verbal, will Dexter win the suit?
31. If the agreement was in writing, had Stan intended to install the new roof?
32. Was the snowstorm anticipated?

Set 6

Facts: Ricky, Lucy, Ward, and June shared a vacation condominium on Lake Tahoe for two weeks each summer. This summer, Ricky and Ward bickered constantly about whether each was shouldering his fair share of the expenses. The argument became more intense one evening while the women were away, and Ward knocked out Ricky in a fistfight. When the women returned, Ward was returning from the lake, and Ricky was nowhere to be found. When asked by Lucy about Ricky's whereabouts, Ward merely grumbled incoherently. Immediately Lucy accused Ward of drowning Ricky and hit Ward with a fireplace poker, causing severe head injuries. Suddenly Ricky staggered out of the bedroom, suffering from nothing more than a severe headache.

Dispute: Lucy was charged with the crime of battery. Lucy contested.

Rule I: Battery is the intentional causing of bodily harm to another.

Rule II: Battery is the causing of bodily harm to another that must take place in the presence of a witness who is not involved in the act of bodily harm.

Questions:

33. Was June still in the same room when the act occurred?
34. If Lucy accidently hit Ward with the fireplace poker and no witness was present, will she be found guilty of battery?
35. If Lucy intentionally hit Ward but there was no witness, will Lucy be guilty of battery?
36. If June was also involved in the act of bodily harm to Ward and was the only witness present to the intentional striking of Ward, will Lucy be found guilty?
37. If the bodily harm to Ward was intentional and June watched in awe but did nothing and was not involved, will Lucy be found guilty of the crime of battery?
38. If there was a witness present, was Ward guilty of battery in his fistfight with Ricky?
39. If Lucy had struck Ward with her fist instead of the fireplace poker, would Ward have been as badly injured?

STOP. IF YOU FINISH BEFORE TIME IS CALLED, CHECK YOUR WORK ON THIS SECTION ONLY. DO NOT WORK ON ANY OTHER SECTION IN THE TEST.

SECTION III: ANALYTICAL REASONING

Time: 35 Minutes
27 Questions

DIRECTIONS

You will be presented several sets of conditions. A group of questions follow each set of conditions. Choose the best answer to each question, drawing a rough diagram of the conditions when necessary.

Questions 1 through 7 refer to the following statements

X, Y, and Z are three chemical elements.
If X reacts with X, the result is Y.
If X reacts with Z, the result is X.
If Y reacts with any element, the result is always Y.
If Z reacts with Z, the result is Z.
The order of the reaction makes no difference.

1. Which of the following must be true?

    I. If X reacts with any other element, the result is never X.
    II. If Z reacts with any element, the result is that element.
    III. If Y reacts with Y, the result is X.

    (A) I   (D) I and II
    (B) II   (E) II and III
    (C) III

2. If the result is Y, then

    I. Y had to be in the reaction
    II. Z had to be in the reaction

    (A) I
    (B) II
    (C) either I or II but not both
    (D) both I and II
    (E) neither I nor II

3. If the result of X and Z reacts with the result of Y and Z, then the result is

(A) X   (D) X or Z
(B) Y   (E) cannot be determined
(C) Z

4. Which of the following must be false?

I. Whenever an element reacts with itself, the result is the original element.
II. If the result is Z, then Z had to be in the reaction.

(A) I
(B) II
(C) either I or II but not both
(D) both I and II
(E) neither I nor II

5. If the result is X, then

I. X had to be in the reaction
II. Y could not be in the reaction
III. Z had to be in the reaction

(A) I   (D) II and III
(B) I and II   (E) I, II, and III
(C) I and III

6. If the result of X and X reacts with the result of Z and Z, then the result is

(A) X   (D) X or Y
(B) Y   (E) cannot be determined
(C) Z

7. A new element W is introduced. When element W is added to any reaction, then the result is W, except when it reacts with Y, the result is Y. If the result of W and Z reacts with the result of W and Y, then the result is *not*

(A) X   (D) X or Y
(B) Y   (E) W, X, or Z
(C) Z

Questions 8 through 13 refer to the following statements

Twenty books are stacked evenly on four shelves, as follows:
There are three types of books: science fiction, mystery, and biography.
There are twice as many mysteries as science fictions.
All four science fiction books are on shelf number 2.
There is at least one mystery on each shelf.
Shelves numbers 3 and 4 have equal numbers of mystery books.
No shelf contains only one type of book.

8. Shelf number 3 has

   I. at least one mystery book
  II. no science fiction books

  (A) I
  (B) II
  (C) both I and II
  (D) either I or II but not both
  (E) neither I nor II

9. Which of the following must be true?
  (A) No shelf has more than two mysteries.
  (B) No shelf has more than two biographies.
  (C) There is never only one mystery on a shelf.
  (D) There is never only one biography on a shelf.
  (E) There are always more mysteries than biographies on a given shelf.

10. If the books on shelves numbers 1 and 4 are put together, then

    I. they must contain equal numbers of mysteries and biographies
   II. they contain no science fiction
  III. they contain over half of the biographies

  (A) I   (D) I and II
  (B) II   (E) II and III
  (C) III

11. All of the following are true *except*
    (A) shelf number 2 contains no biographies
    (B) shelf number 3 contains no science fiction
    (C) shelf number 4 contains equal numbers of each book
    (D) shelf number 1 could contain mostly mysteries
    (E) shelf number 3 could contain three biographies

12. Shelf number 4 must have
    (A) four mysteries
    (B) two different types of books, in the ratio of 3 to 2
    (C) two different types of books, in the ratio of 4 to 1
    (D) all three different types of books, in the ratio of 2:2:1
    (E) cannot be determined

13. Shelf number 1 must have
    (A) two different types of books, in the ratio of 3 to 2
    (B) two different types of books, in the ratio of 4 to 1
    (C) three different types of books, in the ratio of 2:2:1
    (D) four mysteries
    (E) none of the above

Questions 14 through 18 refer to the following statements

The government is arranging an expedition to an under-developed area of the world and has to select a four-member team. Two of the members must be engineers. The following professionals applied for the expedition:

A is an architect.	E is an engineer.
B is a biologist.	F is a field engineer.
C is a chemist.	G is a general engineer.
D is a doctor.	

The architect and the engineer will not go together.
The doctor and the general engineer will not go together.
The biologist and the architect will not go together.

14. If A is selected, the rest of the expedition would be composed of
    (A) C, D, and F   (D) C, E, and F
    (B) B, F, and G   (E) E, F, and G
    (C) C, F, and G

15. If the field engineer is rejected, then the others rejected would be
    (A) the chemist only
    (B) the chemist or the biologist
    (C) the architect, chemist, and engineer
    (D) the architect and doctor
    (E) the biologist, chemist, and doctor

16. If the general engineer is selected, then which of the following must be true?

    I. The biologist is selected.
    II. The architect is not selected.

    (A) I only
    (B) II only
    (C) both I and II
    (D) either I or II but not both
    (E) neither I nor II

17. Which of the following must be true?

    I. G and A can never be on the expedition together.
    II. C and E can never be on the expedition together.
    III. F and C will always be on the expedition together.

    (A) I   (D) all of these
    (B) II   (E) none of these
    (C) III

18. If the doctor is selected and the chemist is not selected, then the expedition will be composed of
    (A) A, E, and F   (D) B, E, and G
    (B) B, E, and F   (E) A, B, and F
    (C) A, F, and G

Questions 19 through 24 refer to the following statements

Al, Paul, Jim, Sam, and Bob have an average height of six feet.
Sam is taller than Al.
Bob is shorter than Jim.
Paul is shorter than Sam.
Bob is taller than Paul.
Sam is shorter than Jim.
Paul is the shortest of the five.

19. The tallest man is
    (A) Al
    (B) Bob
    (C) Sam
    (D) Jim
    (E) cannot be determined

20. Al is not necessarily
    I. taller than Paul
    II. taller that Bob

    (A) I only
    (B) II only
    (C) either I or II
    (D) both I and II
    (E) neither I nor II

21. Which of the following must be true?
    I. Jim is taller than Al.
    II. Sam is taller than Bob.
    III. Bob is taller than Al.

    (A) I
    (B) II
    (C) III
    (D) I and II
    (E) II and III

22. If Harold joins the group and is taller than Bob, but shorter than Al, then which of the following must be true?
    I. Sam is taller than Harold.
    II. Al is taller than Bob.

(A) I only   (D) both I and II
(B) II only   (E) neither I nor II
(C) either I or II

23. If Tom joins the group and is taller than Bob, then Tom is
    (A) shorter than Al
    (B) taller than Al
    (C) shorter than Sam
    (D) taller than Sam
    (E) cannot be determined from the given information

24. If Ernie joins the group and is the same height as two of the other men, then
    (A) Sam is the same height as Al
    (B) Al and Bob must be the same height
    (C) Sam and Bob must be the same height
    (D) Bob must be the same height as Ernie
    (E) this is not possible from the given information

Questions 25 through 27 refer to the following statements

    Doctors X, Y, and Z can treat diseases L, M, N, and O.
    Doctor X can treat only one disease.
    Doctor Y cannot treat disease M.
    Disease O cannot be treated by Doctor Z.
    Diseases L and O are treated by the same doctor.

25. Which of the following must be true?

    I. Doctor Z treats disease L.
    II. Doctor X treats disease O.

    (A) I only
    (B) II only
    (C) both I and II
    (D) either I or II but not both
    (E) neither I nor II

26. Which of the following must be false?

   I. Disease N cannot be treated.
   II. Doctor Y treats only one disease.

   (A) I only
   (B) II only
   (C) both I and II
   (D) either I or II but not both
   (E) neither I nor II

27. Which doctor could treat the most diseases?
   (A) Doctor X
   (B) Doctor Y
   (C) Doctor Z
   (D) They could all treat the same number of diseases.
   (E) It cannot be determined.

STOP. IF YOU FINISH BEFORE TIME IS CALLED, CHECK YOUR WORK ON THIS SECTION ONLY. DO NOT WORK ON ANY OTHER SECTION IN THE TEST.

SECTION IV: READING COMPREHENSION

Time: 35 Minutes
27 Questions

DIRECTIONS

Each passage in this group is followed by questions based on its content. After reading a passage choose the best answer to each question and blacken the corresponding space on the answer sheet. Answer all questions following a passage on the basis of what is *stated* or *implied* in that passage. You may refer back to the passage.

Questions 1 through 7 refer to the following passage

The field of sociology in the United States developed as a result of a social experience which had very little to do with the political and ideological controversies that stimulated sociology in France and Germany. Rather, the discipline evolved as a result of the experiences associated with the problems of an immigrant society caught in the turmoil of rapid industrialization and urban growth. Indeed, it must be emphasized that from its beginnings, sociology has had a very practical interest, which was characterized less by political divisiveness than by social reform and social work. This practical emphasis in the discipline has continued to persist to the present. It has only been since World War II, however, that there has existed something in American higher education that could be properly termed a "sociological establishment" or a highly respected academic field of study. Its major strength as an academic discipline resulted from its empirical and sophisticated approach to the identification and solution of practical but highly significant social problems.

Today, what does the academic sociologist do? Professional sociologists are individuals who study and teach about societies, social institutions, and the patterns of human interaction and human behavior. As a scientific discipline, sociology may be divided into three broad, analytical fields: the study of groups; institutional analysis; and the study of the social structure in general. Thus, the content of the rapidly expanding discipline of sociology is based upon culture and society, with emphasis placed upon the study of the various types of interaction and relationships which exist among individuals and human groups. In the study of such areas as social organization and disorganization, sociologists attempt to explain the evolution and change of social institutions and the changing nature of human attitudinal and value systems. Among the selected topics of investigation included within the study of sociology are the changing nature of family life, institutional life, sexual attitudes, crime and violence, religious values, and the entire gamut of interpersonal relationships in politics and government. Indeed, many of the areas which professional sociologists study are, by their very nature, relatively familiar to many of us even though they are not clearly understood. The basic hypotheses of the discipline— that social life (both group and individual behavior) is patterned; that values and attitudes are learned, reinforced, and shared; that we as individuals are, in many respects, what others consider us to be—are ideas which most people now instinctively accept in order to live and function as members of society. These topics, which emphasize individual and group behavior processes, then, comprise the areas of concern for sociology as one of the behavioral science disciplines.

During these last decades of the twentieth century, advanced Western society will continue to be confronted with crucial social issues in the context of both individual and group behavior patterns resulting from continued rapid technological expansion. The solutions to the problem plaguing our complex society will become, to a much greater extent, the primary responsibility of sociology, social psychology, and cultural anthropology, the three major academic disciplines comprising the behavioral sciences. This trend is being witnessed currently by the increasing numbers of behavioral scientists that are being employed by government, by business and industry, by hospitals and other agencies devoted to problems of health care, by welfare agencies, by public educational systems, and by many other types of organizations in which some systematic knowledge of human behavior is required.

1. The primary purpose of the passage is to
   (A) distinguish sociology in the United States from sociology in France and Germany
   (B) compare sociology with social psychology and cultural anthropology
   (C) provide a general discussion of modern Western sociology and its significance
   (D) distinguish academic sociologists from professional sociologists
   (E) show that sociology is the study of social institutions

2. With which of the following statements about sociology would the author be most likely to disagree?
   (A) Most sociologists are interested in theoretical rather than practical questions.
   (B) Sociology in France and Germany grew out of political and ideological causes.
   (C) One's self-image is not encoded genetically.
   (D) There is a discernable structure to everyone's behavior.
   (E) Human behavior can be systematically studied.

3. It can be inferred from the passage that social psychology and cultural anthropology
   (A) are subareas of sociology
   (B) are scarcely relevant to the future problems that sociologists will encounter
   (C) will achieve the academic respectability of sociology
   (D) may be consulted for solutions to sociological problems
   (E) are other names for sociology

4. Which of the following is the most appropriate title for this passage?
   (A) Behavioral Sciences
   (B) An Overview of Sociology
   (C) The Sociologist in the Twentieth Century
   (D) Sociology and Behavior
   (E) The Sociology of Groups and Individuals

5. The author would most likely agree with which of the following statements?
   (A) Sociology theory is rarely based on empirical evidence.
   (B) The problems facing sociologists do not change as times change.
   (C) There are factors in interpersonal relationships that are not of interest to the sociologist.
   (D) The interests of the group are more important than the interests of the individual.
   (E) The problems of immigrants in a new culture stimulate sociological research.

6. The passage supplies information in answer to which of the following questions?
   (A) What are some solutions to future sociological problems?
   (B) What do sociologists generally study?
   (C) Which sociological theories influence modern practice most strongly?
   (D) Why didn't the "sociological establishment" fully emerge until after World War II?
   (E) How can a sociologist utilize psychological and sociological evidence?

7. The final sentence of the passage implies that
   (A) sociology will overtake other academic disciplines
   (B) the goal of both business and government is a systematic knowledge of human behavior
   (C) certain behavioral scientists are employed in both the public and private sectors
   (D) behavioral science is studied and practiced outside an academic context
   (E) there are increasing job opportunities for behavioral scientists

Questions 8 through 14 refer to the following passage

One of the basic test procedures used to evaluate hearing is the puretone audiometric test. Puretone audiometry consists of presenting the listener with a series of calibrated pure tones at different frequencies and intensities. An extensive discussion of the acoustic components of a pure tone is beyond the scope of this passage. Simply, a pure tone consists of a stimulus with a known frequency, intensity, and phase. The tones are produced by an audiometer. The intensity of the pure tones can be manipulated through an attenuator, which is similar to a volume control switch on a radio. The goal is to determine the least (softest) amount of intensity needed to obtain a predetermined response. Briefly, the procedure consists of presenting the tone at an intensity sufficiently loud for the listener to hear it. He is asked to respond, typically by raising his hand, each time he hears the tone. The tone is then systematically decreased in intensity until the listener no longer indicates that he hears it. This is referred to as obtaining a listener's threshold for pure tones.

The standardized equipment needed to appropriately administer a puretone threshold test is a puretone audiometer. Several suitable units are available commercially. They may range from a portable model to more elaborate console models. The type of audiometer employed will depend upon the user's goals. However, all units must fulfill certain standard requirements as stipulated by the American National Standards Institute in their reported entitled "American National Standards Specifications for Audiometers." Some of the pertinent requirements stipulated in this report for an acceptable puretone audiometer to be used for clinical diagnostic testing include definite specifications concerning the (1) test tones (frequencies) to be included, (2) reference level for normal hearing at each frequency (sound-pressure levels [SPL] as designated by ANSI, 1969), including upper and lower SPL ranges and a hearing threshold level dial calibrated in 5 decibels or less, and (3) minimum specifications for a tone interrupter switch and masking noise.

In order to obtain a valid threshold measure for pure tones, testing must be administered in a relatively quiet setting. In other words, the environmental noise levels in the room selected for testing must be sufficiently low (quiet) so as not to interfere with hearing the test tone when the hearing threshold level dial is set at 0 decibels Hearing Threshold Level. The American National Standards Institute (ANSI) has published criteria (including maximum allowable ambient noise levels) in order to obtain a 0 decibel screening level with a normally hearing person wearing standard earphones in the selected test site. This information is outlined in a booklet entitled *The American National Standard Criteria for Background Noise in Audiometer Rooms.*

Special soundproof treatment of most existing rooms is almost always required even when they are subjectively judged quiet and away from other possible or intermittent external noises. It is often necessary, therefore, to purchase prefabricated hearing testing rooms that have been designed specifically for the purpose and provide the desirable noise reduction (attenuation) needed for valid testing.

The noise levels of rooms being considered as hearing testing sites can be checked against the ANSI criteria through the use of sound measuring equipment, such as a sound-level meter and frequency analyzers. Consequently, there is little reason to be testing in an inadequate environment.

There are several procedural considerations to be made when searching for a listener's threshold. These include (1) the length of time the tone is presented to the listener, (2) the length of time between tone presentations, (3) whether the tone progressed from audibility to inaudibility or in reverse order, and (4) the kind of listening instructions given. Each of these factors can alter the threshold obtained.

8. The author provides information about which of the following aspects of the puretone audiometric test?

   I. equipment used in testing
  II. preferable environment for testing
 III. the steps to be followed during the testing procedure

    (A) I only
    (B) II only
    (C) I and II only
    (D) II and III only
    (E) I and III only

9. Which of the following best characterizes the author's tone?
   (A) uninterested   (D) objective
   (B) argumentative   (E) cavalier
   (C) subjective

10. By *threshold* the author means
    (A) the maximum capacity of the attenuator
    (B) the maximum capacity of the puretone audiometer
    (C) the special soundproofing surrounding the edges of the door in the testing room
    (D) the maximum intensity that the human ear can endure
    (E) the decibel level at which the listener can no longer hear a pure tone

11. Which of the following conclusions can be inferred from the final paragraph of the passage?
    (A) The acoustic components of a pure tone are complex.
    (B) Those who administer the test sometimes give imprecise instructions.
    (C) A listener's threshold is not invariable.
    (D) Each listener's threshold should be measured several times.
    (E) Scientific equipment is not always reliable.

12. We may infer from the passage that a listener's perception that the testing room is quiet may be
    (A) an educated guess
    (B) unreliable
    (C) verified by asking other listeners
    (D) limited by national standards
    (E) influenced by national standards

13. The primary purpose of this passage is to
    (A) indicate the proper environment for hearing tests
    (B) describe the types of equipment used for hearing tests
    (C) develop a working definition for normal hearing
    (D) convince a lay audience of the value of audiometric testing
    (E) explain various aspects of the puretone audiometric test

14. The author would probably agree with which of the following conclusions?
   (A) Hearing impairment is detectable only through the controlled administration of the puretone audiometric test.
   (B) Calibrated equipment yields accurate information under widely varying circumstances.
   (C) The primary goal of any hearing evaluation procedure is to obtain consistent responses to known auditory messages that are presented to the listener in a standardized manner.
   (D) The puretone audiometric test detects only one type of hearing disorder.
   (E) Good equipment and adequate environment are more important for audiometric testing than are trained personnel.

Questions 15 through 20 refer to the following passage

Each method of counting bacteria has advantages and disadvantages; none is 100 percent accurate. Cell counts may be made with a counting chamber, a slide marked with a grid to facilitate counting of cells and to determine the volume of liquid in the area counted. Counts are made under a microscope and calculations made to determine the number of cells per ml of the original culture. Electronic cell counters can be used to count cells suspended in a liquid medium which passes through a hole small enough to allow the passage of only one bacterial cell at a time. The counter actually measures the rise in electric resistance of the liquid each time a cell passes through the hole. Smear counts are similar to cell counts: a known volume of culture is spread over a know area (1 cm^2) of a slide and then stained. Counts are made from several microscope fields, and calculations are made. In membrane filter counts a known volume of a culture is passed through a filter, which is then examined microscopically for cells. The advantage of cell counts, smear counts, and membrane filter counts is that they are quickly accomplished with little complicated equipment; however, both living and dead cells are counted.

The serial-dilution method involves the making of a series of dilutions, usually by a factor of 10, into a nutrient medium. The highest dilution producing growth gives a rough indication of the population of the original culture; for example, if the highest dilution to produce growth is the 1:100 dilution, the original culture had between 100 and 1,000 cells per ml.

Plate counts are made by making serial dilutions (usually in sterile tap water or an isotonic solution) of the original culture. Samples of known volume of the dilutions are transferred to petri dishes and mixed with nutrient agar. After a suitable incubation period the colonies on the plates with between 30 and 300 colonies are counted. Because each colony is assumed to have arisen from a single cell, calculations can be made to determine the original population size. Plate counts have the advantage of not including dead cells, and they can be used when the population is so low as to make other methods impractical, but they require more time than direct counts, and they detect only those organisms that can grow under the conditions of incubation; the development of one colony from more than one cell is also a source of error. In connection with this technique a modification of the membrane filter count can be used. After filtration, the filter is placed on a pad soaked in nutrient media and allowed to incubate; resulting colonies are counted and appropriate calculations made.

A colorimeter or spectrophotometer is used in turbidimetric methods; the instrument measures the amount of light transmitted by test tubes with and without cultures; the difference represents the light absorbed or scattered by the bacterial cells and gives an indication of their concentration.

The total cell volume in a sample can be determined by centrifuging the sample in a calibrated centrifuge tube. From the known volume of a single cell and the volume of the sample cells, the original population size can be calculated.

The dry weight of washed, dehydrated cells gives a reliable indication of population size. Chemical assays for the concentration of nitrogen or other cell constituents present in cells in fairly constant amounts are used to calculate population size. Because living cells produce chemical changes in their environments, these changes may reflect the number of cells present; changes in pH or in the concentration of a substrate or product may be measured.

In a typical growth curve there is no increase in number of viable cells in the lag phase, but the cells increase in size, imbibe water, and synthesize enzymes as they become adjusted to the new medium. This phase is long if the inoculum consists of dormant cells and/or cells that were previously cultivated on a different medium. Dormant cells have fewer ribosomes than actively growing ones, and some time is required for the formation of ribosomes on which enzymes are then synthesized.

In the logarithmic phase the growth rate is most rapid, and the length of the generation time is at its minimum. The growth rate is constant. This portion of the curve plots as a straight line on semilogarithmic paper. Cells are physiologically active; their characteristic biochemical abilities are most obvious at this time. Almost all cells in the culture are alive, and the population is more nearly uniform than in any other phase of the growth curve. As logarithmic growth proceeds, the food supply diminishes and waste products accumulate.

At the stationary phase the food supply has fallen to a limiting concentration and the waste products have reached an inhibiting concentration. There is no change in the number of viable cells; the production of new cells is balanced by the deaths of other cells. The growth rate is zero, but the population size is at its highest level, called the maximum crop.

During the death phase the number of viable cells decreases as the number of deaths surpasses the number of new cells produced—slowly at first, then more rapidly. The number of viable cells decreases at a logarithmic rate. The length of the death phase varies with the species. It may be only a few days in the case of some gram-negative cocci, but for most species it lasts a few weeks or even months.

Cells can be maintained indefinitely in a logarithmic phase by continuously adding nutrients and removing toxic metabolic products and excess cells in a siphon overflow. The growth rate is controlled by the rate of introduction of fresh medium. Because the overflow contains cells as well as waste products, the population size remains constant.

15. One method of counting bacteria which does not suffer from a major disadvantage of a "cell count" is a

(A) plate count   (D) serial-dilution count

(B) smear count   (E) down for the count

(C) membrane filter count

16. The lag phase is the time during which
    (A) some cells multiply faster than others which "lag" behind
    (B) cells nourish themselves, grow, and eventually reproduce
    (C) cell population is stable
    (D) actively growing cells contribute ribosomes to dormant ones
    (E) adjustment to the new environment is negligible

17. According to the passage, the typical result of incubation is
    (A) impractical
    (B) the precise population of the original culture
    (C) mutation of the nutrient agar
    (D) growth
    (E) 30 to 300 colonies

18. One of the characteristics of the logarithmic phase might be described as
    (A) physiological stasis
    (B) ennervation
    (C) mitosis
    (D) conspicuous consumption
    (E) the recycling of waste products

19. The passage allows us to conclude that a biologist in a hurry to do a bacterial count might choose to
    (A) seek out a spectrophotometer
    (B) estimate the total cell volume
    (C) perform a smear count
    (D) incubate
    (E) use a petri dish

20. During which phase is the population size described with a term commonly applied to agricultural production?
    (A) stationary phase
    (B) lag phase
    (C) logarithmic phase
    (D) death phase
    (E) harvest phase

Questions 21 through 27 refer to the following passage

Man has probably always been curious about himself. We can surmise that primitive man's dependence upon his environment would not have permitted him to be indifferent to the effects of his surrounding world upon him. Very early in the history of mankind the living things which shared his world, especially other humans, must have aroused in him a special interest. He must have speculated on their behavior and how he was alike or different from them. It is easy to imagine his asking the familiar questions "What am I?" "How did I come to be what I am?"

We suspect that somehow he stumbled upon the notion of attributing spirits to things that moved as an explanation for their motion. This *animistic* belief system was applied to fire, water, clouds, plants, or to anything which moved. The conclusion that the leaf falls from the tree because the spirit of the leaf or the tree caused it to move may lead us to smile, but animism was important as a first step man took toward understanding nature.

Similar explanations are provided by young children. When the child sees that the trees move when the wind blows, he may come to believe that trees make the wind blow; thus, he is attributing volition to the trees. Although his premise, and consequently his conclusions, are inaccurate, he is seeking causality, which too is an important first step.

It is not implausible to infer that early man eventually accepted the anthropomorphic viewpoint that his behavior as well as that of all animals was accounted for in terms of purposive inner agents or spirits. From the immobility after death, for example, it was assumed that the spirit had left. This spirit which lacks physical dimensions came to be known as the soul, or "psyche" in Greek, the word from which psychology derives its name.

In time every aspect of behavior was attributed to a corresponding feature of the mind or inner person. To some the inner man was seen as driving the body, much as a person drives a car, and speculation on the nature of this inner person or personality was given considerable attention. Furthermore, how the "mind" or inner man related to the physical body and its actions became an important point of departure for those seeking answers to man's nature. The first conjectures about this relationship were recorded by philosophers, eventually becoming known as the "mind-body problem."

Gradually in the course of inquiring into the nature of the universe by ancient philosophers, there arose the question "How can we know?" In other words, how can we be sure any knowledge is valid? Later this concern for validity led to inquiries into the question "How *do* we know?"—the processes of knowledge. Very early philosophers had distinguished between knowledge gained by the senses and knowledge achieved by reason. They had noted, too, that knowledge is *human* knowledge and therefore influenced by human ways of knowing. The question which arises next is whether any human mode of conceiving the world can have objective validity; whether inquiring into the ultimate nature of reality is not, after all, quite futile.

Socrates considered the effort futile. But he believed that one kind of knowledge is obtainable—knowledge of the self. This kind of knowledge is needed because it will reveal man's duty and enable him to lead a virtuous life. Socrates believed that virtue is the outcome of knowledge and that evil is fundamentally ignorance. This is an early instance of the belief that the intellectual or rational is dominant in man and morally superior.

21. The primary purpose of this passage is to
    (A) speculate about the validity of ancient theories of being
    (B) refute the premise that people are not curious about themselves
    (C) show that the earliest beliefs about human nature and knowledge were naive and childlike
    (D) survey ancient viewpoints on human nature and human knowledge
    (E) argue that ancient speculations about human nature culminated in the philosophy of Socrates

22. Which of the following assumptions underlies the author's statement that animistic beliefs were "inaccurate"?
    (A) There is no superhuman spirit in the universe.
    (B) The movement of inanimate objects is always caused by some external force.
    (C) Modern speculations about causality are accurate.
    (D) Ancient thinkers did not think carefully about causality.
    (E) The animistic belief system is only practiced by creatures of a lower order than human.

23. Which of the following questions is (are) answered by information in the passage?

    I. Can any human mode of conceiving the world have objective validity?
   II. Was Socrates virtuous?
  III. Is epistemology, the study of knowledge, an exclusively modern interest?

    (A) I and III only   (D) III only
    (B) II and III only   (E) I only
    (C) II only

24. Socrates' point of view, as described in the passage, implies which of the following conclusions about evil people?
    (A) They are ignorant.
    (B) They are unable to achieve complete self-knowledge.
    (C) They are inherently virtuous, but incapable of showing it.
    (D) They are often either ignorant or irrational.
    (E) They often dominate those who are morally superior.

25. The "mind-body problem," as described in the passage, is based upon which of the following assumptions?
    (A) Only when separated do the mind and body present no problem.
    (B) All outward appearance reflects the inner person.
    (C) While the body may change, the mind remains essentially unchanged.
    (D) No aspect of physical behavior is a purely physical reflex action.
    (E) "Mindlessness" is impossible.

26. From the passage, we may conclude about the author's knowledge of the origins of the animistic belief system that he or she
    (A) concludes that animism is a direct answer to the question, "What am I?"
    (B) views animism as an outgrowth of earlier belief systems
    (C) is certain that animistic beliefs were acquired by accident
    (D) is not sure what the origins were
    (E) suspects that animism is not a step toward understanding nature

27. Which of the following definitions of *psychology* best reflects the ancient Greek notion of *psyche*, as explained in the passage?
    (A) the study of the mind-body problem
    (B) the study of the mind
    (C) the study of the soul
    (D) the study of life after death
    (E) the study of human behavior

STOP. IF YOU FINISH BEFORE TIME IS CALLED, CHECK YOUR WORK ON THIS SECTION ONLY. DO NOT WORK ON ANY OTHER SECTION IN THE TEST.

SECTION V: LOGICAL REASONING

Time: 35 Minutes
26 Questions

DIRECTIONS

You will be presented with brief passages or statements and will be required to evaluate their reasoning. In each case, select the best answer choice, even though more than one choice may present a possible answer. Choices which are unreasonable or incompatible with common-sense standards should be eliminated.

Questions 1 and 2 refer to the following passage

The new vehicle inspection program is needed to protect the quality of the state's air, for us and for our children. Auto exhausts are a leading contributor to coughing, wheezing, choking, and pollution. The state's long-term interests in the health of its citizens and in this area as a place to live, work, and conduct business depend on clean air.

1. Which of the following, if true, would most seriously weaken the argument above?
   (A) Since smog devices were made mandatory automotive equipment by the existing inspection program three years ago, pollution has decreased dramatically and continues to decrease.
   (B) Pollution problems are increasing in other states as well as in this one.
   (C) Sometimes coughing, wheezing, and choking are caused by phenomena other than pollution.
   (D) Vehicle inspectors are not always careful.
   (E) The state should not impose its interests upon the citizenry but should instead allow public health to be regulated by private enterprise.

199

2. Which of the following is an unstated assumption made by the author?
   (A) Working and conducting business may be different activities.
   (B) The state has been interested in the health of its citizens even before this inspection program was proposed.
   (C) Exhaust emissions contribute to pollution.
   (D) The new inspection program will be effective.
   (E) Our ancestors did not suffer from air pollution.

We doubt that the latest government report will scare Americans away from ham, bacon, sausages, hot dogs, bologna, and salami or that it will empty out the bars or cause a run on natural food supplies. If a diet were to be mandated from Washington, Americans probably would order the exact *opposite* course. Therefore the diet that does make sense is to eat a balanced and varied diet composed of foods from *all* food groups and containing a reasonable caloric intake.

3. Which of the following is (are) specifically implied by the passage?
   I. Vitamins are necessary to combat disease.
   II. A recent report warned of the risks of meat and alcoholic beverages.
   III. Unorthodox suggestions for a more nutritional diet were recently made by the government.

   (A) I only   (D) I and II
   (B) II only   (E) II and III
   (C) III only

In his first message to Congress, Harry Truman said, "The responsibility of the United States is to serve and not dominate the world."

4. Which of the following is one basic assumption underlying Truman's statement?
   (A) The United States is capable of dominating the world.
   (B) The United States chooses to serve rather than dominate the world.

(C) World domination is a virtue.

(D) One must be decisive when facing a legislative body for the first time.

(E) The United States, preceding Truman's administration, had been irresponsible.

Without sign ordinances, everyone with the price of a can of spray paint can suddenly decide to publicly create their own personal Picassos, and soon the entire town would start to look like something out of *Alice in Wonderland*. Therefore we need sign ordinances.

5. The author makes which of the following basic assumptions?

   I. Spray paint is used for many signs.

  II. The entire town looking like *Alice in Wonderland* is undesirable.

 III. Sign ordinances are effective.

(A) I only   (D) I and III

(B) II only   (E) I, II, and III

(C) III only

> **Speaker:** One need not look very far to find abundant examples of incivility and brutality in the most genteel corners of American society.
>
> **Questioner:** Then why don't we step up law enforcement in the slums of our cities?

6. The question reveals which of the following misunderstandings?

(A) the misunderstanding that incivility and brutality have become more abundant

(B) the misunderstanding that law enforcement is related to the problems of incivility and brutality

(C) misunderstanding of the speaker's position relative to incivility and brutality

(D) misunderstanding of the meaning of the word *genteel*

(E) misunderstanding of the meaning of the words *incivility* and *brutality*

Experience shows that for every burglar shot by a homeowner there are many more fatal accidents involving small children, family slayings that could have been avoided but for the handy presence of a gun, and thefts of handguns by the criminals they are intended to protect against.

7. Which of the following facts, if true, would most seriously weaken the above contention?
   (A) Criminals tend to sell the handguns they steal during the commission of a burglary.
   (B) Burglars are also capable of causing fatal accidents.
   (C) Every burglar shot by a homeowner is stopped from committing scores of further burglaries and injuring scores of other citizens.
   (D) The number of burglars shot by homeowners is larger than the number of burglars shot by renters.
   (E) Not all fatal accidents involve guns.

Questions 8 and 9 refer to the following passage

Voters on June 8 approved a $495 million bond issue for a state prison construction that is an obvious priority. Now the legislature has voted to put five more general obligation bond issues on the November ballot, adding another $1.5 billion to the states long-term debt. Those on the November menu include $500 million for building and remodeling public schools, $450 million to extend the veterans home loan program, $200 million to subsidize low-interest mortgages for first-time home buyers, $85 million to acquire land for environmental protection, and $280 million to help counties expand or remodel their jails.

8. Which of the following statements is a point to which the author is most probably leading?
   (A) Two of these bond issues are certainly more important than the others.
   (B) We must face the obvious conclusion that prison construction is much less important than the improvement of public education and social programs for lawful citizens.
   (C) The cost of these bond issues is, on the face of it, negligible.

(D) The voters cannot be expected to help make financial decisions for the state because most voters are suffering from their own severe financial problems.

(E) These five bond proposals are quite enough, and between now and November voters will have to study them carefully to make sure that five are not too many.

9. Which of the following facts would most strongly weaken an argument for approval of the five new bond issues?

(A) Environmental protection is not an overriding concern of the constituency.

(B) The state's long-term debt cannot lawfully exceed $1.5 billion.

(C) Improvements in education, the environment, criminal prosecution, and the real estate market are favored by the voters.

(D) Similar bond proposals in other states have not been successful.

(E) Two bills related to the housing of criminals are quite enough.

Famous painter James Whistler said, "Industry in art is a necessity—not a virtue—and any evidence of the same, in the production, is a blemish, not a quality."

10. Whistler is arguing that

(A) of necessity, art becomes industrialized

(B) the qualities of art are its virtues

(C) blemished paintings are the work of overindustrious artists

(D) the product reflects the means of production

(E) the artist must work hard, but the art should look easy

Deliberations of our governing bodies are held in public in order to allow public scrutiny of each body's actions and take to task those actions which citizens feel are not, for whatever reason, in their best interests.

11. With which of the following statements would the author of the above passage probably agree?
    (A) Deliberations of our governing bodies should be held in public.
    (B) Public scrutiny usually results in the criticism of our governing bodies.
    (C) The best interests of the public usually do not coincide with the motives of our governing bodies.
    (D) No government decisions ought to be kept from the public.
    (E) Citizens in other countries are not cared for by the government.

Questions 12 and 13 refer to the following passage

Recent studies indicate that more violent crimes are committed during hot weather than during cold weather. Thus, if we could control the weather, the violent crime rate would drop.

12. The argument above makes which of the following assumptions?
    I. The relationship between weather conditions and crime rate is merely coincidental.
    II. The relationship between weather conditions and crime rate is causal.
    III. The relationship between weather conditions and crime rate is controllable.

    (A) I and II
    (B) II and III
    (C) I, II, and III
    (D) I only
    (E) II only

13. The argument would be strengthened if it pointed out that
    (A) the annual crime statistics for New York are higher than those for Los Angeles
    (B) in laboratory tests, increased heat alone accounted for increased aggressive behavior between members of the test group
    (C) poor socioeconomic conditions, more uncomfortable in hot weather than in cold, are the direct causes of increased crime
    (D) weather control will be possible in the near future
    (E) more people leave their doors and windows open during hot weather

The state's empty $4 million governor's mansion on the banks of the Capitol River may be sort of a suburban Taj Mahal, as the governor once said. Buy why shouldn't the state unload it?

14. Which of the following is one of the author's basic assumptions?
    (A) The governor's mansion is out of place in the suburbs.
    (B) The reader is aware of the state's intention to "unload" the governor's mansion.
    (C) No one has yet lived in the governor's mansion.
    (D) The state is trying to sell the governor's mansion.
    (E) The governor was correct.

All triangles are two-dimensional.
All squares are two-dimensional.
All triangles are squares.

15. This logic would be valid if
    (A) only squares are two-dimensional
    (B) only triangles are two-dimensional
    (C) some triangles are two-dimensional
    (D) some squares are two-dimensional
    (E) some squares are three-dimensional

Questions 16 and 17 refer to the following passage

There was a time, not so long ago, when major public figures in the United States were glad merely to have the opportunity to speak before prestigious national organizations such as the American Bar Association. In that time, expenses might or might not have been reimbursed, and if an honorarium was offered, many public figures would ask that it be given to a charity.

16. The above passage most logically precedes which of the following statements?
    (A) Now public officials can command four-figure fees for speaking.
    (B) Now honoraria are rarely offered, and speakers often appear for no compensation.
    (C) The American Bar Association has been involved in various controversies over the years.
    (D) There was also a time, very long ago, when national organizations had no use for public speakers.
    (E) Some charities manage their money well, while others do not.

17. Which of the following, if true, would most seriously weaken the author's implied point in the above statement?
    (A) Charities rarely receive the honoraria offered to speakers.
    (B) Prestigious national organizations have decreased sharply in number since 1975.
    (C) Present economic problems make it impossible for many national organizations to reimburse their speakers.
    (D) Very few public figures request compensation for their speeches these days.
    (E) Today charities request money from public figures rather than waiting until it is offered.

It is never easy to draw a line between what ought to be mandated by law and what should remain optional in public safety, including the way automobiles are designed and the way they are driven. The issue of overregulation in our society often turns on deciding where common sense leaves off and the law should step in.

18. The statement above follows logically from which of the following statements?
    (A) Historically, parents have lacked sufficient concern for the safety of small children in automobiles and have resisted legislative efforts to mandate the use of special "kiddie seats."
    (B) Those who manufacture and market car seats for small children strongly support legislation that would make the use of such seats mandatory.
    (C) Common sense tells most American parents that the chances for an auto accident to occur are slim and that their children are relatively safe most of the time.
    (D) Parents are taking an increasing interest in protective car seats for their small children at the same time that Congress is considering a bill mandating a special "kiddie seat" restraint for children.
    (E) Because automobiles are private property, the government has no right to regulate their design or use.

Questions 19 and 20 refer to the following passage

We have nothing to fear but fear itself? Nonsense. Even the bravest of us may become terrified in the face of any number of gravely threatening situations.

19. To accept this author's argument, we must agree that becoming afraid is
    (A) an occasional trait of the fearless
    (B) fearful
    (C) a common and acceptable human quality
    (D) nonsense
    (E) allowable only in gravely threatening situations

20. The author's argument might be weakened by pointing out that
    (A) a less fearful attitude may minimize the threat of a situation
    (B) fear promotes more accurate responses to threatening situations
    (C) any blanket generalization is highly vulnerable to criticism
    (D) who we fear is more important than what we fear
    (E) brave people often admit that they have been afraid

21. When Louis Pasteur said, "Chance favors the prepared mind," the famous French scientist most nearly meant
    (A) take a chance only if you're prepared
    (B) pasteurization was a chance that Pasteur prepared for
    (C) being prepared will be favorable to those who take chances
    (D) happenstance will be more beneficial to those who are prepared
    (E) we all have a chance to be prepared

22. Which of the following most logically completes the passage at the blank below?

    Filmmakers tend to highlight their emotional points with visuals, rather than dialogue. Words tend to be the tools of playwrights. Images are the stuff that films are made of. Nevertheless, many successful films have been made from stage plays and contain little else than one location or one stage set. It would seem, then, that films _____.

    (A) are not necessarily a filmmaker's medium
    (B) are not limited to any one particular style
    (C) are solely built upon visual and eye-catching scenes
    (D) are better made by playwrights and novelists
    (E) perhaps are better understood by literary critics

    Clammo, the new pocket-sized earplugs, will keep those noisy distractions down! Bothered by office noise? Annoyed by that someone's loud radio? Use Clammo to lessen distractions.

Clammo earplugs fit easily into any size ears and adjust to any situation. Inexpensive, there is nothing else on the market quite like them. Give 'em a try!

23. All of the following are claims made by Clammo except
    (A) affordability   (D) silencing
    (B) convenience   (E) uniqueness
    (C) flexibility

1. A sensible, equitable alternative would be to fund these nonessential courses from fees charged to those who enroll.
2. Granted, these courses are popular, especially with citizens less interested in a degree than in pursuing avocations.
3. The government is paring its budget by dropping hundreds of classes from the state college curriculum—classes in such subjects as aviation, surfing, and fly casting.
4. But is it really necessary for hard-pressed taxpayers to foot the bill for courses that can fairly be described as frills?

24. Which is the most logical order for the above statements?
    (A) 1, 2, 3, 4   (D) 3, 4, 2, 1
    (B) 1, 3, 2, 4   (E) 3, 2, 1, 4
    (C) 3, 2, 4, 1

Questions 25 and 26 refer to the following passage

All acts have consequences. Given this fact, we may wish to play it safe by never doing anything.

25. The speaker implies that
    (A) we may prefer to live safely
    (B) all acts have consequences
    (C) consequentiality is not safe
    (D) doing nothing has lesser consequences
    (E) not doing anything is not an act

26. What conclusion about consequences must we accept if we accept the speaker's statement?
    (A) Consequences are significant only for active people.
    (B) All consequences are dangerous.
    (C) There are some acts that do not produce consequences.
    (D) Consequences have moral force.
    (E) Inaction has moral force.

STOP. IF YOU FINISH BEFORE TIME IS CALLED, CHECK YOUR WORK ON THIS SECTON ONLY. DO NOT WORK ON ANY OTHER SECTION IN THE TEST.

SECTION VI: ANALYTICAL REASONING

Time: 35 Minutes
26 Questions

DIRECTIONS

You will be presented several sets of conditions. A group of questions follows each set of conditions. Choose the best answer to each question, drawing a rough diagram of the conditions when necessary.

Questions 1 through 8 refer to the following passage

1. Liquid A mixes with liquid B to produce liquid C.
2. Liquid C mixes with liquid D to produce liquid E.
3. Liquid A mixes with liquid D to produce liquid F.
4. Liquid B mixes with liquid E to produce liquid A.
5. Liquid F mixes with liquid C to produce liquid B.
6. Liquid E mixes with liquid F to produce liquid D.

1. Which of the following must be true?

   I. Each liquid can be produced by mixing two other liquids.
   II. A mixture of any two liquids will not produce one of the original liquids used in the mixture.

   (A) I only
   (B) II only
   (C) both I and II
   (D) either I or II but not both
   (E) neither I nor II

2. Which of the following could be true but isn't necessarily true?

   I. Liquid B mixes with liquid C to produce liquid A.
   II. Liquid E mixes with liquid F to produce liquid D.

   (A) I only
   (B) II only
   (C) both I and II
   (D) either I or II but not both
   (E) neither I nor II

211

3. Which of the conditions can be deduced from conditions 1 and 2?

(A) 3
(B) 4
(C) 5
(D) 6
(E) none of these

4. From the information given, to produce liquid B (somewhere during the process), we must have

I. liquid F
II. liquid C

(A) I only
(B) II only
(C) both I and II
(D) either I or II but not both
(E) neither I nor II

5. If the product of liquids A and B is mixed with the product of liquids E and F, the resulting liquid is

I. one of the original liquids used
II. not one of the original liquids used

(A) I only
(B) II only
(C) both I and II
(D) either I or II but not both
(E) neither I nor II

6. If the product of liquids C and F is mixed with the product of liquids B and E, the resulting liquid is the same as the one produced by mixing

(A) A and B
(B) B and C
(C) C and D
(D) D and E
(E) E and F

7. If liquid A mixes with liquid F, the product is liquid

(A) A
(B) B
(C) C
(D) D
(E) cannot be determined

8. If three liquids are mixed, the liquid produced is always the same as merely mixing the first and last liquids used; therefore
   (A) if A, C, and E are mixed they produce C
   (B) if A, B, and F are mixed they produce B
   (C) if E, F, and C are mixed they produce A
   (D) if A, B, and D are mixed they produce F
   (E) if B, D, and F are mixed they produce B

Questions 9 through 14 refer to the following passage

1. Three sportswriters predicted winning teams for the four games played over the weekend.
2. Stevens predicted that the Packers, Rams, Bears, and Redskins would win.
3. Cardenas predicted that the Raiders, Bears, Jets, and Packers would win.
4. Blume predicted that the Redskins, Packers, Cowboys, and Jets would win.
5. The Colts played in one of the four games but were not picked to win by any of the sportswriters.
6. The Cowboys and Raiders played on different days.
7. The Rams played the Jets.

9. Using only statements 1, 2, and 3, the Rams could play the
   (A) Packers   (D) Redskins
   (B) Bears   (E) any one of these
   (C) Raiders

10. The only team picked to win by all the sportswriters was the
    (A) Bears   (D) Packers
    (B) Cowboys   (E) Redskins
    (C) Jets

11. If the Colts win, then which of the following must lose?
    (A) Jets   (D) Raiders
    (B) Bears   (E) Packers
    (C) Cowboys

12. Which of the following must be true?

   I. The Cowboys play the Raiders.
   II. The Bears play the Redskins.

   (A) I only
   (B) II only
   (C) either I or II but not both
   (D) both I and II
   (E) neither I nor II

13. If the Jets and Cowboys win, then which one of the sportswriters alone must have predicted the most winners?
   (A) Stevens
   (B) Cardenas
   (C) Blume
   (D) two of the above
   (E) cannot be determined

14. Which of the following must be false?

   I. The Bears play the Cowboys.
   II. The Redskins play the Rams.
   III. The Colts play the Packers.

   (A) I only   (D) I and III
   (B) II only   (E) II and III
   (C) III only

Questions 15 through 21 refer to the following passage

   1. Five planets—A, B, C, D, and E—are orbiting around a central sun, each in its own circular orbit but not necessarily in that order.
   2. The smallest orbit is not planet A's or planet B's.
   3. Planet D has the largest orbit.
   4. Planet C is not in an orbit next to planet E's or D's.
   5. Planet E is closest to the sun.

15. Which of the following must be true?

    I. Planet C is not second from the sun.
    II. Planet D's orbit is next to planet E's.

    (A) I only
    (B) II only
    (C) both I and II
    (D) either I or II but not both
    (E) neither I nor II

16. Which of the following must be false?

    I. The orbit of planet D is between planet C's and planet E's orbits.
    II. The orbit of planet B is between planet C's and planet E's orbits.

    (A) I only
    (B) II only
    (C) both I and II
    (D) either I or II but not both
    (E) neither I nor II

17. From statements 1 and 2, it can be deduced that
    (A) planet B is farthest from the sun
    (B) planet C's orbit is next to planet A's orbit or planet B's orbit
    (C) planet D is farther from the sun than planet B
    (D) planet B's orbit is not next to planet A's orbit
    (E) planet A is not closest to the sun

18. From statements 1 and 5, which statement(s) could have been deduced?

    I. 2
    II. 3
    III. 4

    (A) I   (D) I and II
    (B) II   (E) II and III
    (C) III

19. If planet B's orbit is next to planet C's, then which of the following could be true?

   I. Planet B's orbit is next to planet D's orbit.
   II. Planet A's orbit is next to planet D's orbit.

   (A) I only
   (B) II only
   (C) both I and II
   (D) either I or II but not both
   (E) neither I nor II

20. If planet A's orbit is next to planet E's, then
   (A) planet D's is next to planet E's
   (B) planet B's is next to planet D's
   (C) planet C's is next to planet E's
   (D) planet A's is between planet C's and planet D's
   (E) planet B's is between planet C's and planet A's

21. If planet F is discovered in a circular orbit around the sun and the orbit is next to C's, then planet F's orbit must be

   I. between planet B's and planet C's
   II. between planet A's and planet C's
   III. next to planet E's orbit

   (A) both I and II
   (B) either I or II but not both
   (C) both I and III
   (D) either I or III but not both
   (E) both II and III

Questions 22 through 26 refer to the following passage

In a wagering system payoffs are equal to the amount wagered. After each winning wager, you increase your wager by one unit. After each losing wager, the following wager will be double the one just lost.
The initial wager is two units.

22. If you should lose your first four consecutive wagers, how many units are you losing?

    (A) 8   (D) 64
    (B) 16   (E) none of these
    (C) 32

23. If you should win your first two consecutive wagers, then lose your next two consecutive wagers, what would be your next wager?

    (A) 8   (D) 32
    (B) 16   (E) none of these
    (C) 17

24. If you should lose your first two consecutive wagers, then win your next two consecutive wagers, how many units are you ahead or behind?

    (A) behind 2   (D) ahead 3
    (B) behind 4   (E) ahead 11
    (C) even

25. If you should win your first wager, then lose, lose, win, win, and lose in that order, which of the following would be true?

    I. You will have lost more units than you won.
    II. Your next wager will be ten units.
    III. You will be ahead four units.

    (A) I   (D) I and II
    (B) II   (E) none of these
    (C) III

26. Continuing in problem 25, what would your next (seventh) wager be?

    (A) 14   (D) 28
    (B) 15   (E) 29
    (C) 30

STOP. IF YOU FINISH BEFORE TIME IS CALLED, CHECK YOUR WORK ON THIS SECTION ONLY. DO NOT WORK ON ANY OTHER SECTION IN THE TEST.

ANSWER KEY FOR PRACTICE TEST 2

Section I Logical Reasoning	Section II Dispute Characterization		Section III Analytical Reasoning
1. E	1. D	21. B	1. B
2. B	2. A	22. D	2. E
3. C	3. B	23. C	3. B
4. B	4. C	24. B	4. A
5. E	5. C	25. B	5. E
6. A	6. A	26. A	6. B
7. E	7. B	27. A	7. E
8. B	8. C	28. C	8. C
9. E	9. D	29. B	9. D
10. E	10. A	30. C	10. E
11. E	11. D	31. D	11. C
12. C	12. B	32. D	12. B
13. D	13. B	33. B	13. E
14. B	14. C	34. C	14. C
15. C	15. A	35. A	15. D
16. D	16. B	36. A	16. E
17. E	17. C	37. C	17. E
18. E	18. D	38. D	18. B
19. A	19. B	39. D	19. D
20. E	20. B		20. B
21. D			21. A
22. C			22. D
23. D			23. E
24. D			24. D
25. D			25. E
26. B			26. C
			27. B

ANSWER KEY FOR PRACTICE TEST 2

Section IV Reading Comprehension	Section V Logical Reasoning	Section VI Analytical Reasoning
1. C	1. A	1. A
2. A	2. D	2. A
3. D	3. B	3. E
4. B	4. A	4. C
5. E	5. E	5. A
6. B	6. D	6. A
7. D	7. C	7. E
8. C	8. E	8. D
9. D	9. B	9. C
10. E	10. E	10. D
11. C	11. A	11. E
12. B	12. E	12. E
13. E	13. B	13. E
14. C	14. B	14. B
15. A	15. A	15. A
16. C	16. A	16. A
17. D	17. D	17. E
18. D	18. D	18. A
19. C	19. C	19. D
20. A	20. A	20. B
21. D	21. D	21. B
22. C	22. B	22. E
23. D	23. D	23. B
24. A	24. C	24. E
25. D	25. E	25. C
26. D	26. B	26. D
27. C		

HOW TO SCORE YOUR EXAM

Your score on the actual LSAT is simply the number of questions you answered correctly (minus a small adjustment factor) scaled to a 10–48 scoring range. There is no penalty for incorrect answers other than no credit.

ANALYZING YOUR TEST RESULTS

The charts on the following pages should be used to carefully analyze your results and spot your strengths and weaknesses. The complete process of analyzing each subject area and each individual problem should be completed for each Practice Test. These results should then be reexamined for trends in types of errors (repeated errors) or poor results in specific subject areas. THIS REEXAMINATION AND ANALYSIS IS VERY IMPORTANT TO YOU: IT SHOULD ENABLE YOU TO CONCENTRATE ON YOUR AREAS OF WEAKNESS.

PRACTICE TEST 2: ANALYSIS SHEET

	Possible	Completed	Right	Wrong
Section I: Logical Reasoning	26			
Section II: Dispute Characterization	39			
Section III: Analytical Reasoning	27			
Section IV: Reading Comprehension	27			
Section V: Logical Reasoning	26			
Section VI: Analytical Reasoning	26			
OVERALL TOTALS	173			

WHY?????????????????????????????????

ANALYSIS—TALLY SHEET FOR PROBLEMS MISSED

One of the most important parts of test preparation is analyzing why you missed a problem so that you can reduce the number of future mistakes. Now that you have taken Practice Test 2 and corrected your answers, carefully tally your mistakes by marking them in the proper column.

	Total Missed	Simple Mistake	Misread Problem	Lack of Knowledge
Section I: Logical Reasoning				
Section II: Dispute Characterization				
Section III: Analytical Reasoning				
Section IV: Reading Comprehension				
Section V: Logical Reasoning				
Section VI: Analytical Reasoning				
OVERALL TOTALS				

REASON FOR MISTAKE

Reviewing the above data should help you determine WHY you are missing certain problems. Now that you have pinpointed the type of error, focus on avoiding your most common type.

ANSWERS AND COMPLETE EXPLANATIONS
FOR PRACTICE TEST 2

SECTION I: LOGICAL REASONING

1. (E) This choice raises the question relevant to establishing the mural as art in Aristotelian terms.

2. (B) The first speaker puts forth a "perfect" view of friendship (idealistic), and the second questions the endurance of friendship (cynicism).

3. (C) Answering (A) or (D) requires the unsupported assumption that the 1933 minimum wage was too low and unfair to the workers. The statement describes a circumstance in the past which is obviously much different from present circumstances, thus suggesting choice (C).

4. (B) The conclusion that highway deaths will be reduced with the advent of automatic restraints is necessarily based upon the assumption that such restraints reduce highway deaths. None of the other choices focuses on the conclusion; (E) is an assumption which could motivate the passage as a whole, rather than just the conclusion.

5. (E) Choices (C) and (D) do not address the comparison between journalists and bank employees; and (A) and (B) use the comparison in statements irrelevant to the points in the passage. (E) criticizes the term that links bad journalists with bad bank employees—embezzlement—by pointing out that bank embezzlement does not so dierctly affect the customers of a bank in the same way as biased or false journalism affects the customers (readers) of a newspaper.

6. (A) *Heart and soul* is a metaphor, employing terms normally associated with another subject, humans, to refer to a nonhuman entity, business.

7. (E) This choice is related most fully to the subject matter of the original statement.

8. (B) This suggests that exterior forces, such as advertising, influence consumer choices and undercuts the contention that consumers know what they want. Each of the other choices is either irrelevant or strengthens rather than weakens the argument.

9. (E) Choices (A), (C), and (D) are irrelevant to the argument, and (B) actually strengthens the argument. (E) suggests that the evidence from one year cannot reliably predict a long-term trend.

10. (E) This is implied in the final sentence. Each of the other choices requires assumptions or beliefs extraneous to the passage.

11. (E) I and III. Neither consumers nor legal loopholes are mentioned in the statement.

12. (C) Voltaire's statement shows the irony that the descriptive word used (*common*) may not, in reality, be so. Likewise, the adjective describing the shrimp (*jumbo*) indicates that the shrimp are large; this may not be the case.

13. (D) Making *only* the first word of sentence 1 does not solve all of the logical problems in the passage but does strengthen the passage by indicating that customers with green necklaces must have bought them from the competition.

14. (B) The author does not realize that customers not wearing green necklaces may have bought other items from the competition.

15. (C) The passage establishes that the survivors were caught in a life and death "survival" situation. While (B) may be a possible choice, answer (C) logically follows the sense of their dilemma, clouded by uncertainty and the possibility of death.

16. (D) The letter fails to note that the decision concerns *officers,* and Smith and Krunkle have been merely nominated to be officers and are not yet such. The other choices are either not stated in the letter or are not essential to the argument.

17. (E) Answers (B), (C), and (D) are only partial descriptions and, although may be correct, are not as complete a description of possible future action as answer (E). Nothing in the letter would imply the action stated in (A).

18. (E) Flamo Lighters claim to be convenient ("in your pocket wherever you go"), have longevity ("ten-year guarantee"), winter-

proof ("all-weather"), and dependable ("always reliable, always dependable"). They do not profess to be all-purpose, however.

19. (A) What is graceful and pleasing to the eye is "in the eye of the beholder," something quite subjective. While (B), (C), and (D) are possibly subjective statements, they would not be if their basic assumptions were proven—that is, that reporters do have a commitment, that poverty is a terrible affliction, and that the records are open to question; (A) is the best answer because it is the most identifiably subjective. In addition, only choices (A) and (E) use a clear *comparison*.

20. (E) The cost of a product may not be relevant to its quality. The amount we pay for Japanese televisions has only remote bearing on the quality of American goods in general.

21. (D) *Doubtful* and *open to question* mean nearly the same thing.

22. (C) All race-car lovers enjoy classical music. Since there are no backgammon players who enjoy classical music, then none of the backgammon players are race-car lovers. (D) is false because statement 3 does not necessarily exclude those who don't enjoy classical music from enjoying fine wine.

23. (D) This passage implies that the lie detector is sometimes worthless. If the lie detector can be fooled in certain instances, then in those instances it is worthless.

24. (D) The argument is "It has been *proven* that the 'lie detector' can be fooled." The best choice is the one which provides such proof—(D). (A) and (B) are too general, and (C) weakens the argument.

25. (D) Only this choice both represents a *strong* point *and* is not contradictory. (A), (C), and (E) contradict the argument, and (B) is not a relatively strong point.

26. (B) The argument mentions the reduced quality of a nationally prominent outdoor attraction and advocates its protection. Only (B) makes a similar argument about a similar phenomenon.

SECTION II: DISPUTE CHARACTERIZATION

Set 1

1. (D) The number of viewers watching the endorsements is not an essential issue in the dispute. This question is irrelevant.

2. (A) Each rule leads to a different outcome. By Rule I Porton will lose the suit because he used false advertising. But by Rule II Porton will win the suit because his misrepresentation was unintentional. Since there is no reason to use one rule over the other, a choice is necessary.

3. (B) Since misrepresentation for profit is an essential part of Rule II, this is a relevant question. The facts, however, do not clarify if Porton did stand to profit from the arrangement. Therefore more facts are necessary.

4. (C) If Porton stood to profit from his falsehoods and his misrepresentations were intentional, both rules lead to his being found guilty.

5. (C) This question is quite relevant to the case and is easily answered. No, Porton's statements were not true if refined sugar is not considered a natural ingredient.

6. (A) Both rules lead to different outcomes for this question. By Rule I Porton would be found guilty. By Rule II he would not. There is no reason to use one rule over the other. A choice is necessary.

7. (B) This is an important issue that needs additional information.

Set 2

8. (C) This relevant question is readily answerable from the facts and Rule II. Since the property was not owned by the brewing company, Rule I does not apply. By Rule II he will lose.

9. (D) This question is irrelevant.

10. (A) To answer this relevant question, we must choose between the rules. By Rule I the brewing company is liable and Fred would win, but by Rule II Fred is liable.

226

11. (D) Whether Fred or Mitch caused the accident is irrelevant.

12. (B) This relevant question refers to the ability to use Rule I, but additional facts are necessary.

13. (B) This question is unanswerable without additional facts but is relevant to Rule I.

14. (C) This relevant question can be answered by the application of Rule II. The Beerbelly Brewing Company will win. Rule I does not apply if the entrance was adequate.

Set 3

15. (A) This is a relevant question which requires a choice between the rules. By Rule I Ready Electronics would be found guilty of misrepresentation. By Rule II Ready Electronics would be found not guilty. There is no reason to use one rule over the other. Therefore a choice is necessary.

16. (B) Since the value of the HMB has bearing on the outcome by Rule II, it is a relevant question. However, additional facts are necessary to determine the value.

17. (C) If the HMB was valued at $300 and the misrepresentation was intentional, both rules lead to the same answer: Leslie will win. Note that since the HMB was valued at under $400, the claims need not be in writing to constitute misrepresentation.

18. (D) This question is irrelevant. Whether Leslie ultimately obtained the position at Standard University is not important to the outcome of this case.

19. (B) If the store manager did not intentionally misrepresent, then by Rule I Leslie will not win. Rule II, however, does not address *intentional* misrepresentation. It concerns the value of the item and whether the misrepresentation was in writing. These elements are important to the outcome by Rule II but were not clarified in the facts. Therefore more information is needed.

20. (B) The existence of written representation is essential to the outcome by Rule II. Therefore this is a relevant question for which more information is necessary.

Set 4

21. (B) This relevant question cannot be answered without knowing if the agreement was in writing. Additional facts are necessary.

22. (D) This question is irrelevant.

23. (C) This relevant question can be answered by applying the rules. According to each rule, she will get a refund.

24. (B) This question is relevant to application of each of the rules but needs additional facts to be answerable.

25. (B) This question is relevant to the possible application of Rule I. Additional facts are needed for an answer.

26. (A) To answer this relevant question we need to choose between the rules. By Rule I, since the tires cost under $100, the contract is not binding; therefore the Club would win. By Rule II, since there was an addendum in writing, the Club will lose.

Set 5

27. (A) The answer to this relevant question is different depending upon which rule is chosen. By Rule I Stan has no liability. But by Rule II Stan is liable. Since there is no reason to use one rule over the other, a choice is necessary.

28. (C) Both rules give the same answer to this relevant question: Stan did not assume any liability.

29. (B) This is a relevant question which has important bearing on the dispute. It requires additional facts in order to be answered.

30. (C) Both rules give the same answer to this relevant question: Dexter will lose the suit.

31. (D) This is an irrelevant question. Stan's intention to install a new roof has no bearing on the outcome of the dispute as governed by the rules.

32. (D) This is an irrelevant question. Whether or not the snowstorm was anticipated has no bearing on the dispute as governed by the rules.

Set 6

33. (B) This question is relevant but not answerable without additional facts. Since a witness is necessary under Rule II, June's presence is important.

34. (C) This relevant question can be answered by applying the rules. Since the act was not intentional and no witness was present, Lucy will not be found guilty.

35. (A) To answer this relevant question, we must choose between the two rules. By Rule I she will be guilty, but by Rule II, since there were no witnesses, she will not be guilty.

36. (A) To answer this relevant question, we must again choose between the two rules. By Rule I Lucy is guilty, but if June was involved in the act of bodily harm, Rule II says not guilty.

37. (C) This relevant question is readily answerable by applying the facts to both rules. By each rule she is guilty.

38. (D) This question is irrelevant to the dispute as governed by the rules. Ward was not charged with battery.

39. (D) This question is irrelevant. The object used for striking is not an issue nor is the severity of the injury.

SECTION III: ANALYTICAL REASONING

To help answer questions 1 to 7, you may have constructed the following chart.

	X	Y	Z
X	Y	Y	X
Y	Y	Y	Y
Z	X	Y	Z

1. (B) II only must be true. From the chart you will observe that I is false (when X reacts with Z, the result is X) and III is false (when Y reacts with Y, the result is Y). Only II is true.

2. (E) If the result is Y, then X may have been reacting with X, which is neither I nor II. The key words in the statements are "*had* to be." Y and Z *could* be in the reaction but didn't necessarily have to be.

3. (B) The result of X and Z is X. The result of Y and Z is Y. When X reacts with Y, the result is Y.

4. (A) Only statement I is false; when X reacts with X, the result is Y.

5. (E) The only way X may be the result is if X reacts with Z. Thus X and Z both had to be in the reaction, and therefore Y could not be. Statements I, II, and III are true.

6. (B) The result of X and X is Y. The result of Z and Z is Z. Thus the result of Y and Z is Y.

7. (E) Since Y is involved in the reaction, the result must be Y; therefore, it is *not* W, X, or Z. Although answers (A) and (C) contain two of these letters, neither answer is as complete as (E). You could have expanded the chart like this:

	X	Y	Z	W
X	Y	Y	X	W
Y	Y	Y	Y	Y
Z	X	Y	Z	W
W	W	Y	W	W

From the information given for questions 8 to 13, you could have constructed the following charts, which may be helpful in enabling you to answer. (Note that the circled books must be positioned as shown.)

1.	B	B	M	M	(M		1.	B	B	B	B	(M
2.	(S	S	S	S		M)	2.	(S	S	S	S		M)
3.	B	B	B	M		M	or	3.	B	B	M	M	M
4.	B	B	B	M	(M)		4.	B	B	M	M	(M)

8. (C) From the given information, at least one mystery book must be on shelf number 3, and all the science fiction books are on shelf number 2. Thus none can be on shelf number 3.

9. (D) There is never only one biography on a shelf.

10. (E) Shelves 1 and 4 together contain over half of the biographies and no science fiction.

11. (C) There is no possible way that shelf number 4 could contain equal numbers of each book. Since five books are on the shelf, they cannot be evenly divided.

12. (B) Shelf number 4 must contain either three biographies and two mysteries or three mysteries and two biographies. Either way, the ratio is 3 to 2.

13. (E) Shelf number 1 has either four biographies and one mystery or two biographies and three mysteries.

For questions 14 to 18 a simple connection diagram will be helpful. The lines connect those professionals who would not go together.

From the given information the chart is as follows:

14. (C) If A is selected, then F and G are selected, and E and B are not selected. If G is selected, then D is not selected, therefore the team is A, C, F, and G.

15. (D) If the field engineer is rejected, then the engineer and the general engineer are selected, therefore the architect and doctor would be rejected.

16. (E) If the general engineer is selected, then either the engineer or the field engineer is selected. If the engineer is selected, then the biologist is selected, otherwise neither is selected. Therefore, I is not necessarily true. If the engineer is selected, then the architect is not selected. But the engineer is not necessarily selected, therefore II is not necessarily true. The correct answer is (E), neither I nor II must be true.

17. (E) From the diagram, I is not necessarily true, as G and A could possibly go together. II is also not necessarily true. As you can easily deduce from the diagram, C and E could go together. If F goes on the expedition and E goes on the expedition, then B and C or D could go, therefore III is not necessarily true. The correct answer is (E), none of the above.

18. (B) If the doctor is selected, then the general engineer is not selected, and the engineer and the field engineer are selected. If the engineer is selected, then the architect is not selected, and since the chemist is not selected, then the biologist is selected. Therefore the team would consist of the biologist, doctor, engineer, and field engineer or B, D, E, and F. The other three are therefore B, E, and F.

In questions 19 to 24, using greater than (>) and less than (<) symbols will help place the boys in some order.

Sam is taller than Al.
Bob is shorter than Jim.
Paul is shorter than Sam.
Bob is taller than Paul.
Sam is shorter than Jim.
Paul is the shortest of the five.

$S > A$
$B < J$
$P < S$
$B > P$
$S < J$

Now putting this information together gives the following relationships:

$$J > S > A > P$$

$$J > \leftarrow B \rightarrow > P$$

Notice that some of the boys cannot be placed in exact order. This is not necessary to answer the questions.

19. (D) From the diagram, Jim is obviously the tallest.

20. (B) I is false, because Al is necessarily taller than Paul. II is true, because Al and Bob cannot be compared by the information given, therefore Al is not necessarily taller than Bob.

21. (A) From the chart, I is the only true statement, because Jim is taller than Al.

22. (D) If Harold joins the group and is taller than Bob, but shorter than Al, then the order of the boys must be

$$J > S > A > H > B > P$$

From this chart, I and II must be true.

23. (E) Tom may be taller than Bob, but this information does not allow us to place Tom in relation to either Sam or Al.

24. (D) If Ernie joins the group and is the same height as two of the men, then Ernie must be the same height as *either* Bob and Al or Bob and Sam. Therefore Ernie must at least be the same height as Bob.

25. (E) From the information given, you could have constructed either of the following charts to help you answer the questions.

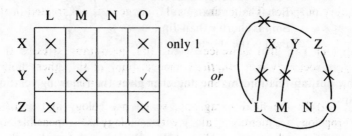

This can be deduced from the statements. Doctor Z cannot treat disease L since Doctor Z does not treat disease O; and Doctor X cannot treat O since Doctor X can treat only one disease (O and L are treated together). Thus, neither statement I nor II *must* be true.

26. (C) Both statements are false. From the information given, we know that all the diseases can be treated. And from our chart, we may deduce that Doctor Y treats at least two diseases.

27. (B) Doctor Y may possibly treat three diseases.

SECTION IV: READING COMPREHENSION

1. (C) Choices (A), (B), and (E) are secondary rather than primary purposes. The distinction (D) suggests is not treated in the passage.

2. (A) The final sentence of the first paragraph stresses that modern sociology is a *practical* science. Each of the other choices reiterates information that the author presents as true.

3. (D) In the final paragraph, social psychology and cultural anthropology are mentioned along with sociology as "responsible" for the solutions of sociological problems; we may infer that these disciplines may be consulted.

4. (B) Each of the other choices is either too specific or too general. The passage surveys sociology in general.

5. (E) Each of the other statements is inconsistent with evidence in the passage; however, (E) reiterates part of the author's initial assertion about sociology stated in the first paragraph.

6. (B) This question is answered at the beginning of the second paragraph. Each of the other questions requires information not supplied by the passage.

7. (D) The final sentence enumerates those areas in which behavioral scientists are employed, and all but one of these areas is outside academia. Choices (C) and (E) are stated rather than implied.

8. (C) Although the final paragraph generalizes about "procedural considerations," the author does not explicitly provide *steps* to be followed.

9. (D) The author presents noncontroversial information in a straightforward way; the purpose is to inform, not to persuade or entertain.

10. (E) As explained in the first paragraph, a threshold is reached when the listener can no longer hear a tone; the second paragraph mentions that threshold level is calculated in decibels.

11. (C) The final paragraph presents factors that can alter the threshold level, thus implying that a listener's threshold is not always the same under all conditions.

12. (B) The fourth paragraph stresses the importance of sound-proofing even when a room has been "subjectively judged quiet," thus implying that such a subjective judgment is unreliable. (A) is also a possible choice, but because the passage does not indicate whether the subjective judgment is "educated" or not, (A) remains a weak answer.

13. (E) Choices (A) and (B) are secondary rather than primary purposes, and (D) and (C) are purposes beyond the scope of the passage.

14. (C) The goal described in (C) is stressed throughout the passage by the author's careful attention to both the nature of the auditory messages presented and the manner in which they should be presented. Each of the other choices either contradicts information in the passage or generalizes beyond the information given.

15. (A) According to the first paragraph, a disadvantage of cell counts, smear counts, and membrane filter counts is that "both living and dead cells are counted." This is not true of plate counts, which "have the advantage of not including dead cells" (paragraph 3).

16. (C) During the lag phase, "there is no increase in number of viable cells." (B) is partially true; it would be correct if not for the claim that cells reproduce.

17. (D) The third paragraph shows that incubation produces colonies, which means that there is population *growth*. Choice (E) describes only the range of colonies which are counted; it is too limited to be the best choice.

18. (D) During the logarithmic phase, "the food supply diminishes" (through consumption, of course), and "waste products accumulate" (conspicuous evidence of such consumption). (A) contradicts the passage, which speaks of the rapid growth rate during this phase.

19. (C) The smear count is one of the methods which is "quickly accomplished." The other choices are related to more time-consuming procedures.

20. (A) During the stationary phase, the highest level of population size is called the "maximum crop." "Crop" is, of course, commonly used as an agricultural term.

21. (D) Each of the other choices is a secondary rather than a primary purpose of the passage. Only (D) reflects the general nature of the passage.

22. (C) A criticism of ancient theories assumes that modern theories are more adequate; otherwise no basis for the criticism exists.

23. (D) The passage certainly raises question I and implies question II but does not answer either of them. By explaining throughout the passage that ancient people were interested in the nature of knowledge, the author indicates that such an interest is not exclusively modern and answers question III.

24. (A) This question draws from a simple, explicit statement in the final paragraph: "Socrates believed . . . that evil is fundamentally ignorance." Each of the other choices is an unwarranted complication or extension of this statement.

25. (D) This choice essentially reiterates the first sentence of paragraph 5, which states the ancient assumption underlying the "mind-body problem."

26. (D) The first sentence of the second paragraph expresses the author's uncertainty about the origins of animism, uncertainty especially apparent in the phrase, "we *suspect* that *somehow* . . ."

27. (C) *Soul* is the definition given for the Greek use of *psyche,* and this leads us to define psychology as the study of the soul.

SECTION V: LOGICAL REASONING

1. (A) The argument for further supervision of vehicle use is most weakened by the statement that present safeguards are already doing the job. (C) and (D) slightly weaken the argument but do not address the overall position of the author.

2. (D) In order to argue for a new inspection program, the author must assume that that particular program, if enacted, will be effective. (C), the only other choice related to the points of the argument, expresses stated information rather than an unstated assumption.

3. (B) Since the author doubts that Americans will stop eating meats or visiting bars, one must conclude that the author is referring to the latest government report warning of the risks of meat and alcoholic beverages. Statement I concerning vitamins may be true, but is not *specifically* implied other than in a very general sense (nutrition). Statement III is not true: there is nothing to suggest that the government report made "unorthodox" suggestions.

4. (A) Truman's statement is not warranted unless one assumes the U.S. capability to dominate the world; that assumed capability makes the choice between serving and dominating possible and is thus a basic assumption.

5. (E) All of the statements are assumptions of the author essential to the argument. The author assumes spray paint to be the medium that graffiti painters use and implicitly abhors the possibility of a town looking like *Alice in Wonderland*. In addition, his or her desire for sign ordinances assumes that they work and are effective in deterring spray painting.

6. (D) The questioner understands the speaker to be referring to a problem restricted to the slums and so does not understand that *genteel* refers to upper-class situations.

7. (C) This choice most directly addresses the argument of the passage. The passage argues that for every burglar shot, there are scores of slayings of the innocent; (C) argues that for every burglar shot, there are scores of prevented slayings.

8. (E) By listing high costs, the author is probably leading to the conclusion that the state's debt is being strained, a conclusion expressed in (E). (C) contradicts the author's emphasis on high costs. (A), (B), and (D) are neither expressed nor implied by the passage; their choice would rely on extraneous assumptions.

9. (B) This fact indicates that the passage of all the bond measures, which would take the debt over $2.5 billion, is illegal.

10. (E) Whistler is saying that constant effort (industry) is necessary but that the artwork (production) should not evidence that effort.

11. (A) By describing in very positive terms the effects of public deliberations, the author suggests the opinion that such deliberations *should* be public.

12. (E) The only correct choice is II; it is argued that hot weather *causes* crime. This is not mere coincidence, and the statement does not state that we *can* control the weather.

13. (B) The argument posits an exclusive relationship between hot weather and crime. (A), (C), and (E) contradict such an exclusive relationship. (D) is irrelevant to the relationship, and (B) provides evidence supporting and strengthening the heat-crime relationship.

14. (B) The author's final question necessarily rests on the assumption that the reader is aware of the state's intention; the author omits information expressing or explaining this intention.

15. (A) Diagrams can sometimes be helpful:

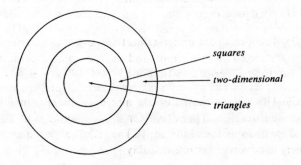

If only squares are two-dimensional and since triangles are two-dimensional, then triangles would have to be squares.

16. (A) The passage stresses a past condition, implying a contrast with a present condition; only (A), (B), and (E) refer to present conditions, and only (A) refers to a *contrasting* present condition.

17. (D) The author's implied point is that the time has passed when speakers appeared for little or no compensation. (D) weakens this point by suggesting that this time has *not* passed.

18. (D) Only choice (D) states specifically the problem that is addressed in the initial statement, implicitly raising the question concerning the relationship between private action and public law. The examples it presents lead to the generalization that this relationship, or conflict, is difficult to resolve. None of the other choices is better because each of them resolves the conflict one way or another, so each is inconsistent with the irresoluteness of the initial passage.

19. (C) By agreeing that fear is acceptable, we can also agree that fearing fear is nonsense. (D), the only other choice that corresponds at all with the argument of the passage, is a weak choice because the author is arguing that fearing fear itself is acceptable.

20. (A) Choices (B) and (E) support the author's argument by stressing further the importance of fear. (C) could either support or weaken the argument, depending upon whether it is taken to refer to the blanket generalization that the author attacks or to the further generalization that the author presents. (D) is irrelevant to the argument, which does not stress the importance of the source of fear.

21. (D) "Chance favors the prepared mind" means that those who are prepared will be "favored" by chance—that is, will be able to take advantage of and most benefit from chance occurrences.

22. (B) The passage juxtaposes visual images with words. Though films tend to be more visual, some successful films have been built primarily on the words of the playwright and don't include exciting visual images. Therefore (C) is incorrect. (D) and (E) are assumptions unsupported by the passage. Choice (A) may be partially correct; however (B) most logically completes the main thrust

of the passage—that is, that films may be solidly built on something other than visual images and thus manifest a different style.

23. (D) Clammo claims to be affordable ("inexpensive"), convenient ("pocket-sized"), flexible ("adjust to any situation"), and unique ("nothing else like them"). While they do claim to minimize noise, they do not profess to provide *silence* for the user.

24. (C) Sentence 3 introduces the college courses explicitly, and 2 logically follows by referring to them as "these courses." Sentence 4 poses a question about the courses that have been implicitly defined as frills in sentence 2, and sentence 1 offers an answer to that question.

25. (E) Choices (A) and (B) are not implied; they are explicitly stated. (C) is vague; the meaning of *consequentiality* is not clear. (D) is incorrect because the author is arguing that doing nothing has no consequences. Choice (E) is correct. This author says that doing nothing keeps us safe from consequences; this could be true only in light of the implication that doing nothing is not an act.

26. (B) According to the author, the alternative to experiencing consequences is playing it "safe." This can mean only that consequences are dangerous.

SECTION VI: ANALYTICAL REASONING

1. (A) From statements 1 to 6, we know that each liquid can be produced by mixing two other liquids (I). By mixing two liquids, however, you *may* get one of the original liquids used in the mixture. Thus statement II could be false.

2. (A) From the information given, you could have constructed this chart to help you answer the questions.

	A	B	C	D	E	F
A		C		F		
B	C				A	
C				E		B
D	F		E			
E		A				D
F			B		D	

or

	A	C	E
B	C	?	A
D	F	E	?
F	?	B	D

From the chart we can see that statement II (E + F = D) *is necessarily* true. But the information does not give us any result for C + B. So C + B = A *could* be true but isn't *necessarily* true.

3. (E) None of the conditions stated allows us to deduce any of the other conditions stated.

4. (C) From statement 5 we know that to produce liquid B we must mix liquid F with liquid C. So at some time during the process we must have both I and II.

5. (A) The product of A and B is C. The product of E and F is D. Thus if the two products are mixed (C and D), our chart shows the resulting liquid to be E, which is one of the original liquids used in the second operation.

6. (A) The product of liquids C and F is B. The product of liquids B and E is A. Mixing these products is the same as mixing A and B.

7. (E) Our chart shows that if liquid A mixes with liquid F, we do not know what the result will be.

8. (D) Since A and D produce F, then A, B, and D will produce F.

Using the information, the following chart or Venn diagram may be constructed which will help answer questions 9 to 14.

	Stevens	Cardenas	Blume
Packers vs. Colts	Packers	Packers	Packers
Rams vs. Jets	Rams	Jets	Jets
Bears vs. Cowboys	Bears	Bears	Cowboys
Redskins vs. Raiders	Redskins	Raiders	Redskins

or

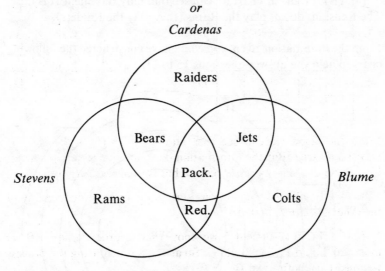

9. (C) Using only statements 1, 2, and 3, we know that two sportswriters both picked the Packers and Bears to win their games. The first sportswriter picked the Rams and the Redskins. Since the other sportswriter picked the Jets or the Raiders, then, necessarily, the Rams must have played either the Jets or the Raiders.

10. (D) Statements 2, 3, and 4 tell us that each sportswriter picked the Packers to win.

11. (E) From the chart we can see that if the Colts win, then the Packers must lose.

12. (E) From the chart we can see that the Cowboys do *not* play the Raiders (they play the Bears), and the Bears do *not* play the Redskins (they play the Cowboys). Thus neither statement I nor II is true.

13. (E) If the Jets and the Cowboys win, then Blume has picked at least two games correctly. Since all the sportswriters picked the Packers, we may discount that game, since it won't have any bearing on who picked the most winners. However, if the Raiders win and the Redskins lose (Blume picked the Redskins), then Cardenas will have predicted as many winners as Blume. Thus we cannot determine which *one* sportswriter alone must have predicted the most winners.

14. (B) From our chart we can see that only statement II is false. The Redskins do *not* play the Rams (they play the Raiders).

From the information given, you could have constructed the following chart to help you answer questions 15 to 21.

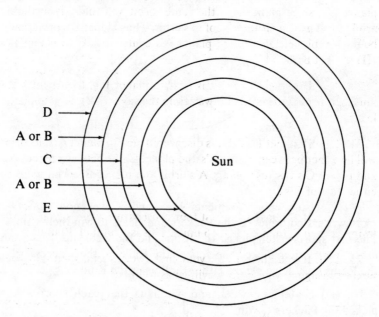

15. (A) Since planet E is closest to the sun and planet C's orbit is not next to planet E's, planet C is not second from the sun. So

statement I is true. Since planet D has the largest orbit and planet E has the smallest orbit, they are on opposite ends and thus their orbits cannot be next to each other. So statement II is false.

16. (A) Since planet D has the largest orbit, it is farthest from the sun and thus its orbit cannot be between the orbits of any of the other planets. So statement I must be false. From the information given we cannot pinpoint planet B's orbit. Planet B's orbit *may* be between those of planets C and E.

17. (E) From statements 1 and 2 we know that neither planet A nor planet B has the smallest orbit. Thus we know that (E), planet A, is not closest to the sun.

18. (A) From statements 1 and 5 we know that planet E is closest to the sun. Thus we then can deduce that 2, the smallest orbit, is not planet A's or planet B's.

19. (D) We already know that planet B's orbit has to be next to planet C's, since planet C is the center orbit and the only available orbits for B are on either side of C's orbit. Thus planet B's orbit could be next to planet D's (I) and planet A's could be next to planet D's (II) but not both.

20. (B) If planet A's orbit is next to planet E's, then planet B's must be the next to last orbit away from the sun, or (B), next to planet D's.

21. (B) If planet F's orbit is discovered next to planet C's, its orbit will lie either between planet B's and planet C's or between planet A's and planet C's because planet A's orbit and planet B's orbit were on either side of C's.

22. (E) If you lose your first four consecutive wagers, you will be losing 2, then 4, then 8, then 16 units. This is a total of 30 units.

23. (B) If you should lose your first two wagers, then win your next two wagers, your wagers will go as follows:

2	3	4	8	16
W	W	L	L	

So your fifth wager would be double your last, or 16 units.

24. (E) If you should lose your first two wagers and then win your next two wagers, your total winnings or losings will be as follows:

$$+2 \quad -4 \quad +8 \quad +9 \quad \text{(or a total of } +11)$$

25. (C) If you should win your first wager, then lose, lose, win, win, and lose, your results would look like this:

$$+2 \quad -3 \quad -6 \quad +12 \quad +13 \quad -14 \quad \text{(or a total of } +4)$$

26. (D) Continuing to wager on problem number 25, since you lost the last wager, you would double the next one, or wager 28 units.

FINAL PREPARATION: "The Final Touches"

1. Make sure that you are familiar with the testing center location and nearby parking facilities.
2. The last week of preparation should be spent primarily on reviewing strategies, techniques, and directions for each area.
3. Don't *cram* the night before the exam. It's a waste of time!
4. Remember to bring the proper materials to the test—identification, admission ticket, three or four sharpened Number 2 pencils, a watch, and a good eraser.
5. Start off crisply, working the ones you know first, and then coming back and trying the others.
6. If you cannot work a problem, at least take an educated guess.
7. Mark in reading passages, underline key words, write out information, draw diagrams, take advantage of being permitted to write in the test booklet.
8. Make sure that you are answering "what is being asked" and that your answer is reasonable.
9. Using the TWO SUCCESSFUL OVERALL APPROACHES (p. 7) is the key to getting the ones right that you should get right—resulting in a good score on the LSAT.